D0053908

DEDICATION

It is our joy to dedicate this book to the partners of our ministry who live in various places throughout the world. Over many years, you have faithfully believed in the assignment the Lord gave to Denise and me, to our sons, and to our team. We have felt your love; we have been recipients of your prayers; and we have been strengthened as you stood with us so many times over the years, showing your support with your financial contributions.

In 1991, God spoke to our hearts and placed His call on our lives to take His Word to what is now the former USSR. But it was a dream far bigger than we were able to fulfill alone — so at the same time God spoke to us, He also put in the hearts of many God-called partners a steadfast desire to help us. Together we have seen miracles, salvations, and the Kingdom advanced for nearly two decades.

Denise and I are thankful for you and hold you dearly in our hearts. You have helped us fulfill the dream God gave us, so it is our joy to dedicate the new edition of this book about fulfilling dreams to you. Many "dream thieves" have tried to stop this work over the years, but by God's grace and with His help, we have pressed ahead and seen Him do remarkable things.

You have been part of God's supernatural grace extended on our behalf, helping us to keep moving forward as we strive to do what Heaven has asked of our family. Thank you for your love and for your partnership in the Gospel of Jesus Christ.

Rick Renner

TABLE OF CONTENTS

CHAPTER FOUR

Sustaining Your Fire
for the Dream in Your Heart

CHAPTER FIVE

A Biblical Patriarch Worth Imitating

INTRODUCTION

When I first wrote this book, it was 1992 and the Soviet Union had just collapsed. My wife Denise and I had obeyed the call of God and moved with our young sons to the crumbling USSR to begin our ministry to that region of the world. Since that time, many years have come and gone, and God has mightily blessed our lives and ministry. Today I'm sitting at my desk in our Moscow home. Our sons grew up in this part of the world and have all married godly and beautiful Russian young women. Denise and I are the proud grandparents of wonderful Russian-American grandchildren. And today God's call is burning in our hearts more strongly and brightly than ever before.

My family and I are here because God spoke to our hearts and gave us a dream about doing a work for Him in this region of the world at this critical time in human history. When God first began to speak to Denise and me about expanding our ministry into this broken land — dominated for so many years by Communism — we had many questions about many important issues. We wondered about our safety, about finances, and about how to conduct our ministry simultaneously on two continents.

I sometimes try to imagine what our lives would have been like had we allowed these questions to direct our path — not to mention all the potential negative scenarios presented to us by the enemy or by well-meaning people. One thing is for sure: If we had listened to the naysayers, we wouldn't be fulfilling God's purposes in the former Soviet Union today. However, with the help of God, those fears, questions, and doubts were pushed aside, and Denise and I wholeheartedly began to pursue the ever-unfolding dream that God has placed in our hearts for reaching the wonderful people who live in the former USSR — most of whom have never heard the Gospel of Jesus Christ and the teaching of God's Word.

I say all of this to let you know that *Dream Thieves* was not born out of a mental exercise or a theoretical examination of Scripture. This book was born out of the challenges my family and I have faced with our own "dream thieves" and out of our own deep desire to fulfill God's will in spite of all opposition.

I've written other books that dealt with specific doctrinal issues in the Body of Christ that needed balance and biblical exposition. This book is far more personal. Within its pages, I discuss the calling, the anointing, and the giftings of God on your life, and I share how you can fulfill the dream God has planted in your heart on your way to your divine destiny.

Therefore, it's my prayer that, as you read this book, God's purpose for your life will be so stirred up within you that you lay aside all your questions and fears and begin to aggressively and unrelentingly pursue whatever He has been telling you to do. If this book encourages you to begin taking the necessary steps on your way to seeing God's plan fulfilled in your life, I will be forever grateful to Him.

Your brother and friend in Jesus Christ,
Rick Renner
Moscow, Russia 2009

CHAPTER ONE

HOLDING FAST

Many people have started out with a God-given dream, and a passion to see that word from the Lord fulfilled in their lives burned in their hearts. But the longer it took for the dream to come to pass, the less their hearts burned for it. Finally, these people released God's dream for their lives altogether, letting it slip out of their hearts and hands and into oblivion. Nothing is more tragic than this: that a person would let go of his dream — the very purpose for which he was born into this world.

You were born to be remarkable! No one else in the world is just like you. Your genetic makeup belongs only to you. Your fingerprints are unlike any others in the entire world. Your blood type, your chemistry, your eye color — all of these are so unique and so special that there isn't any other human being on the face of the earth exactly like you. You are truly one of a kind!

In the same way, your dream — your God-given vision, your word from the Lord — is also unique. God has a special plan for you that is for you alone and no one else. In fact, you are so special and unique that God had His hand on your life even before the foundation of the world (Ephesians 1:4)!

> The greatest tragedy you could ever experience would be to let go of your God-given dream and allow the fire in your heart to go out.

The greatest tragedy you could ever experience would be to let go of your God-given dream and allow the fire in your heart to go out. To do that is the equivalent of letting go of your special individuality, your divine call, and your God-given giftings.

Perhaps you're concerned about being odd or different. But so what if your dream is different than the dreams of other people you know? You must remember that God didn't call you to be conformed to the image of the opinions of your family or friends.

How boring it is to be just like everyone else! You were called to be conformed to the image of Jesus Christ. One of the keys to achieving that goal is to find God's plan for your life and then to follow it to your divine destiny — regardless of the cost.

BE HONEST WITH YOURSELF AND WITH GOD

Years ago when I was ministering at a certain church, the associate pastor asked if he could take me to lunch. While we were eating, this minister began to bare his heart to me. He said, "Rick, I've enjoyed being an associate pastor, but now I sense that God wants me to go out and start my own church. In fact, I'm so consumed with this desire that I'm even dreaming about it at night! Everything in my heart and soul is yearning to have a church of my very own. Do you think it's really God's will for my life?"

As I sat and listened to this man, I could hardly believe his last question, "Do you think it's really God's will for my life?" That man had the pastoral gift oozing out of every cell in his body — yet confusion and doubt were hounding his troubled mind. Several times he asked me, "Do you really think it's God's will, or do you think it's just something *I* want to do? How can I know God's plan for my life?"

By the time our conversation had ended, it had become very apparent to me that this man already knew God's will for his life. What he really needed was a sounding board — someone to whom he could speak his heart and then hear that person say, "You can do it! Go for it!"

Many of us already know the course God wants us to take in our lives. Yet because we haven't learned to discern the hindering, dream-destroying forces that attack our minds, will, and emotions, we retreat from what God has revealed to us and simply watch life pass us by. Meanwhile, we can't stop wondering what would have happened if we'd taken the big leap of faith and done what God told us to do.

Taking the big leap of faith from where you currently are to where God wants you to be can seem like an intimidating and sometimes impossible challenge to your natural eyes. When you begin to lift up your foot to step forward, every part of your soul will scream, *What if you're making a mistake? What if it doesn't work? What will you do then?*

Most people try to ignore or even deny the existence of these questions in their minds. But such questions are natural when a person is thinking about attempting something new in his or her life.

Here's the important thing to remember when those kinds of thoughts are racing through your mind: Instead of hiding from the questions, you need to *answer* them! Prayerfully seek God's wisdom as you look at every question, face every fear, and examine every doubt with total honesty, and don't stop seeking until you know you've heard from Him. Then you can make some strong decisions about your life based on the answers you receive from the Lord.

There's nothing wrong with our taking a good look at a situation before we step out in faith! Even Jesus told us to count the cost before we start a new project.

> **For which of you, intending to build a tower, sitteth not down first, and counteth the cost, whether he have sufficient to finish it? Lest haply, after he hath laid the foundation, and is not able to finish it, all that behold it begin to mock him, saying, This man began to build, and was not able to finish.**
>
> **Luke 14:28-30**

The reason many people fail is not for lack of vision, but for lack of resolve — and *resolve is born out of counting the cost*! It's very easy to start a project, but it's another thing altogether to keep the project going and to stick with it until it is finished. However, if you look at every angle and consider all the aspects of the project before you begin, you will experience fewer shocks and surprises and a lot less stress as you carry out the assignment to completion.

> The reason many people fail is not for lack of vision, but for lack of resolve — and *resolve is born out of counting the cost*!

Many Christians back away from God's call and plan for their lives after considering all the possible challenges they may face. Forging into unknown territory where they've never gone before requires a greater cost than many are willing to pay. They may be bored with their present job, but at least they have job security! They may know in their hearts they were born to achieve more than they're currently achieving — but at least they're comfortable!

The truth is, the Holy Spirit will use any questions, doubts, or fears you may have to incite you to count the cost before pursuing the dream God has put in your heart. For this reason, those questions and doubts are valid and should be dealt with before you make any big change in your life. This process of evaluation isn't to encourage doubt or fear. Rather, it's an important step in developing an inner resolve that will endure, regardless of any obstacles or difficulties you may encounter along the way.

You see, your new course of direction *will* be challenged. Your new career *will* be assaulted. That new concept for your business, your ministry, or your family may cause you to encounter difficulties you've never experienced before. Therefore, rather than moving into this new pursuit blindfolded and ignorant, look at it from beginning to end. Think it all the way through.

Count the cost as Jesus commanded. Your dream stands in danger of perishing if you don't gain the knowledge you need to fulfill it (Hosea 4:6).

Once you've been totally honest with yourself and with God — and perhaps with your spouse and your business or ministry associates — determine whether or not you're still convinced that this new venture is God's will for your life. If so, it's time for you to push aside all fear and doubt and begin to make headway with what He has told you to do.

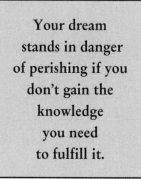

Your dream stands in danger of perishing if you don't gain the knowledge you need to fulfill it.

I remember many years ago when God first called Denise and me to the pastoral ministry. What a challenge that was for me! Not only had I never served in such a capacity, but I also had to be willing to move from the place I'd lived all my life to another state.

Later when that assignment was completed, God spoke to us, telling us to take our teaching ministry to a national level. Again we were challenged to the core! We didn't have a network of ministers to call upon. We had a child, another baby on the way, a house payment, and bills to pay!

In order to step out in faith — and to step out with all our hearts — we had to carefully and cautiously examine the situation, pray diligently about all our questions, and come to a concrete position in God. After examining all the information and godly counsel we could acquire, we came to the conclusion that this was indeed God's plan and that we as a family were willing to do whatever it would take to obey Him. *But we first counted the cost before taking that big step into the next stage of our ministry.*

Then in 1991, God called Denise and me to expand our ministry to what is now the former USSR. Once again we went through the same process of confirming and reconfirming the plan of God in our hearts and souls. It was more than simply a matter of moving our family to the other side of the world. We also had a full staff at our U.S.-based office, all of whom needed to be paid their salaries each month, and an extensive teaching ministry that spanned across the entire United States.

If we were going to take this huge step of faith by moving to the Soviet Union, we would need more finances and more partners. New sacrifices would have to be made by our family and staff members. Many other issues had to be taken into consideration as well. We couldn't just charge ahead without praying and thinking through all these issues, confirming in our hearts that this was truly God's plan for our lives and ministry. Only the hasty and immature would move ahead in such a huge venture without counting the cost first.

But what do you do once the call of God has been confirmed in your heart? What is the next step after your fears have been addressed, your apprehensive thoughts have been answered, and you've made the decision to do whatever is required of you in order to accomplish what God is calling you to do?

At that point, you must set your heart on the assignment God has given you — without budging, hesitating, flinching, or doubting. Once you truly *know* God's will for you, you must follow through by obeying what He's told you to do — no matter what

> Once you truly *know* God's will for you, you must follow through by obeying what He's told you to do — no matter what your friends, your family, or your surrounding circumstances have to say about it!

your friends, your family, or your surrounding circumstances have to say about it!

PRAYERFULLY CONSIDER OPPOSING VIEWS

Please understand — I'm not telling you to rudely ignore what your family and friends say to you, even if they seem to oppose your dream. More than likely, they are speaking out of genuine concern for you and your future. Remember, you were also concerned before you received the answers you were seeking. Even though you know you've heard from God, your loved ones may not have sought God to receive confirmation. Therefore, what seems like opposition may be nothing more than their desire to make absolutely sure you've really heard from the Lord.

Any family member or friend who really loves you would want to make you think once, twice, or even three times about taking a big step of faith before you actually take it. Besides, if someone can talk you out of that decision, perhaps you're not ready to move forward anyway!

Never forget that there is wisdom in godly counsel. If you haven't really heard from God — if you've been led astray by your own understanding or emotions — godly counsel can expose the error and spare you a lot of grief.

SEE THE BIG PICTURE

Here is something else you must understand: There is much more at stake here than a simple desire on your part to do something new or innovative. You need to see the big picture. Although God desires to *use* you, He is much more interested in *changing* you.

> You need to see the big picture. Although God desires to *use* you, He is much more interested in *changing* you.

It's wonderful when God uses us in this earthly realm, but it is also very *temporal*. Our lives on this earth, even with our greatest accomplishments, are but "...a vapour, that appeareth for a little time, and then vanisheth away" (James 4:14). Yes, God wants to use us to carry out His will in the earth, serving as a channel through which His supernatural power can transform the lives of people around us. But that isn't all He wants. As we step out in faith to obey the Lord, trusting Him and choosing to believe His Word over anything and anyone else, we ourselves will also be miraculously changed, transformed from glory to glory into the image of Jesus Christ (2 Corinthians 3:18).

On the other hand, what happens if you sit and stagnate in your comfort zone, refusing to change or to grow, ignoring divine opportunities that God sets before you? When you make that choice, you choose to stay in a place where He is hindered from working in your life.

The Holy Spirit can't give you powerful new revelation from God's Word if you're not accepting the challenges that would require a fresh word from the Lord in order to achieve success. As long as you insist on remaining where you are with no obstacles to overcome, the Holy Spirit will be hindered in His desire to display His delivering power or to bring forth godly character and integrity in your life.

As long as you choose to remain in that place of false security, you will live a mediocre life without a plan or purpose — denying your calling, your giftings, and your potential. Mediocrity will be your standard because you won't allow yourself to develop spiritually. You won't mature in the knowledge of God, nor will you grow in His wisdom.

God knows that you can obey Him only if you are willing to deal with your fears, your unbelief, and your selfishness. This is His prerequisite to your carrying out the dream He has placed in your heart: You must renew your mind to His way of thinking and His way of seeing things. You must be transformed by His Word.

In order for you to fulfill the vision that burns within you — the word you've received from God — He requires that alterations and

> In order for you to fulfill the vision that burns within you — the word you've received from God — He requires that alterations and changes are first made in *you*!

changes are first made in *you*! That, my friend, is exactly what God is after in your life.

You must always keep in mind that your *works* are not the only thing God is concerned about. He is just as concerned with your *character*, your *faith*, and the condition of your *spirit*. These are all aspects of your life that will last for all eternity! God is more passionate about *you* and your willingness to yield yourself wholly to Him than He is about everything you might accomplish in this life.

So when you say, "But this step of faith will demand so many changes in me!" — you're exactly right! That's what God wants to do: He wants to *change* you in the process of *using* you. He wants you to be all you can be in terms of talent, ability, and character. He wants you to be conformed to the image of Jesus Christ, who walked in complete obedience to the revealed will of God for His life.

Don't stop short of the goal. Let the Spirit of God deal with your heart. Let Him reveal the areas of weakness that hinder you. Let Him help you work through your fears and anxieties. Above all, don't deny your individual uniqueness and your irreplaceable part in His great plan. You were created to be remarkable, not just in your achievements, but in the very essence of your being!

FIRMLY EMBRACE GOD'S PLAN FOR YOUR LIFE

In order for you to fulfill the dream God has placed in your heart, it's imperative that you understand Hebrews 10:23, which states, "Let us hold fast the profession of our faith without wavering (for he is faithful that promised)." This scripture can help lay a solid foundation within you, enabling you to accept and carry out the call of God on your life.

I want you to particularly notice the phrase "hold fast." This phrase is taken from the Greek word *katecho*, which is a compound of the two words *kata* and *echo*. The first word, *kata*, carries the idea of something that comes *downward*. You could say that this word conveys *something that comes down so hard and heavily that it is overpowering, dominating, and even subjugating.* When this extremely strong force arrives on the scene, it conquers, subdues, and immediately begins to demonstrate its overwhelming, influencing power.

The second part of the word *katecho* is the word *echo*, which simply means *I have* and carries the idea of *possession*. It is the picture of someone who has sought after a particular item his entire life. After years of seeking, he has finally found what he has been searching for. Joyfully he rushes forward to seize his treasure and hold it tightly. He wraps his arms around the object of his desire, making it his very own, and declares, "I have it!" or "It's finally mine!"

When *kata* and *echo* are compounded into the word *katecho*, the new word doesn't just mean *to embrace*; it actually means *to embrace something tightly*. Because of the word *kata*, we know that this is the image of someone who finds the object of his dreams and then holds it down — even to the point of sitting on it! — in order to dominate and take control of it. If you will do this with the word you've received from God, your dream won't be able to get away from you, nor will anyone be able to take it away!

The phrase "hold fast" conveys such strength that it can actually mean *to suppress something*. In fact, the phrase "hold fast" (*katecho*) is actually translated as the word "suppress" in Romans 1:18 (*NKJV*). Here Paul describes ungodly men "...who suppress the truth in unrighteousness...." Because Paul uses the word *katecho* (suppress), we know that these ungodly men are not ignorant of the truth. They know what is true, but they don't like it! Therefore, rather than allow the truth to get out so it can positively affect people, they "suppress" or "put a lid on" it.

Often the media is told to "sit on a story" rather than publish it because certain influential people don't want the truth to be told so that it gets away from their ability to control it. This is another example of the meaning of *katecho*.

Now this same word, which isused so negatively in Romans 1:18, is used in Hebrews 10:23 to describe the strong response we should have to God's plan for our lives. When we finally discover a portion of God's will for us, His plan begins to awaken in our hearts, and we come to understand what job to take, what business to start, what ministry God has called us to fulfill, and so forth. But if we don't hold fast to our God-given vision, tightly embracing what He has shown us, the "dream thieves" will see to it that we slowly let our dream slip away from us.

This is the very reason we are told to "hold fast" to the word God has spoken to our hearts. We must seize that dream — wrap our arms of faith around it, hold it down, grasp it tightly, and place all our weight on top of it. If we don't, the dream

> If we don't hold fast to our God-given vision, tightly embracing what He has shown us, the "dream thieves" will see to it that we slowly let our dream slip away from us.

thieves of life will come to steal the wonderful plan God has for our lives. If they succeed in doing so, they will steal our uniqueness and our individual purpose in the magnificent plan of God — and nothing would be more tragic than this.

DREAM THIEF NUMBER ONE: *TIME*

We all know that in and of itself, time is a neutral force. Time can work for us or against us; it can be either a healing or a destructive force. For example, we've all heard the saying, "Time heals all wounds." But we've also heard about situations where people sadly remark, "There just wasn't enough time to save them." In each of these situations, time played a very important role, either negatively or positively.

You will face a multitude of dream thieves in life, but *time* is one of the primary strategies Satan uses to try to steal your dreams. There's just something about the passage of time that has a way of gnawing away at your faith and perseverance.

As the months and years pass and your dream remains unfulfilled, the enemy will use the passage of time to bring accusations against you in your mind. He'll whisper: *"You're nothing more than a dreamer! You probably didn't receive a true word from the Lord after all. It was just something you wanted to happen — a wild idea you dreamed up to make you feel more important in your small, insignificant world! You're just a dreamer. So let go of your fantasy, and get back to the real world!"* You may even get to the place where you regret that you ever discovered God's plan for your life.

Perhaps it seems like your entire life has been put "on hold" since the moment you received a word from the Lord about His plans for you. Maybe you've thought about the great life you might be living right now if He had never planted that dream in your heart. You may even be tempted to "kiss it all good-bye" and forfeit the rewards of obedience — just for the sake of a "normal life."

I wonder how many men and women of God have come to this place in their spiritual walk. Having waited so long to see their victory, they regret that God ever spoke to them. Rather than holding down their dream with even more effort and resolve, the passing of time pressures them to let it slip through their fingers. Finally, these believers abandon God's plan altogether. All too often, however, they let go of their dream when they're on the brink of experiencing the full manifestation of His promise in their lives.

First Peter 5:6 tells us, "Humble yourselves therefore under the mighty hand of God, that he may exalt you *in due time.*" Whenever time becomes a dream thief that attempts to steal our God-given vision, we must "hold fast" and remind ourselves again and again that it *will* come to pass "in due time."

> **Whenever time becomes a dream thief that attempts to steal our God-given vision, we must "hold fast" and remind ourselves again and again that it *will* come to pass "in due time."**

We must establish our hearts in the Word of God, refusing to be moved or shaken by the length of time it takes for us to see the fruit of our labor and the manifestation of our steadfast faith. In Chapter Six, we'll discuss in depth the key ingredients that will prevent time from robbing us of our dreams: *faith* and *patience*.

DREAM THIEF NUMBER TWO:
SATAN

If the passage of time doesn't cause you to let go of your dream, you will most certainly begin to hear the sarcastic, condemning voice of the adversary ringing in your ears. The devil will come along to accuse you of being just another run-of-the-mill, ordinary person who is tired of the status quo and doesn't like the direction his or her life has taken. The enemy will point his gnarled finger at you and bombard your mind with his accusations: *"You want to believe that you were born for a special purpose, but you live in a fantasy world. You're just like everyone else, except you have a bigger ego!"*

When Satan starts whispering these kinds of accusations to your mind, he is attacking your very identity in Christ. The devil knows the strategic value of convincing you that the dream for greatness God has placed in your heart is nothing more than a self-exalting "ego trip" and that, in order to be truly humble, you must be and do absolutely nothing in this world. If the enemy can convince you of this lie, he has stolen and obliterated your purpose in life.

Again, we must look to the Word of God for strength of will and steadfastness in the faith. According to Scripture, our destiny was prearranged before the foundation of the world. We are told in the first and second chapters of Ephesians and in the second chapter of First Peter that God foreordained the works in which we should walk and that we are a "peculiar people" who will reveal His glory in the earth.

> **In whom also we have obtained an inheritance, being predestinated according to the purpose of him who worketh all things after the counsel of his own will.**
>
> **Ephesians 1:11**

> **For we are his workmanship, created in Christ Jesus unto good works, which God hath before ordained that we should walk in them.**
>
> **Ephesians 2:10**

> **But ye are a chosen generation, a royal priesthood, an holy nation, a peculiar people; that ye should shew forth the praises of him who hath called you out of darkness into his marvellous light.**
>
> **1 Peter 2:9**

Psalm 139 also tells you that God saw you while you were still in your mother's womb. He watched your body being knit together and ordained your days on this earth before you had lived even one of them!

Your eyes saw my unformed body. All the days ordained for me were written in your book before one of them came to be. How precious to me are your thoughts, O God! How vast is the sum of them! Were I to count them, they would outnumber the grains of sand....

Psalm 139:16-18 *NIV*

Both Jeremiah and the apostle Paul stated that they had been separated from their mother's womb to fulfill the purpose for which God had called them.

Then the word of the Lord came unto me [Jeremiah], saying, Before I formed thee in the belly I knew thee; and before thou camest forth out of the womb I sanctified thee, and I ordained thee a prophet unto the nations.

Jeremiah 1:4,5

But when it pleased God, who separated me [Paul] from my mother's womb, and called me by his grace, to reveal his Son in me, that I might preach him among the heathen....

Galatians 1:15,16

My friend, you are no mistake. Before God ever formed this universe, He had already planned the course for your life. If you haven't yet discovered your divine purpose, the day will come when you will wake up to God's plan — whether it's the day you receive Jesus as your Lord and Savior or years after you are born again. That divine plan will seem new and glorious to *you* — but, in reality, God's purpose for your life has been in existence for eons and eons of time!

> You are no mistake. Before God ever formed this universe, He had already planned the course for your life.

When you follow your dream, all you're doing is plugging into God's plan. When that happens, your life suddenly has meaning and purpose — and you sense an inner excitement you never dreamed possible. *Nothing* is like a dream birthed within your human heart that comes straight from the throne of God!

The devil will try to convince you that this grand and glorious dream is just your own self-exalting fantasy and that God's true plan for your life follows a more "humble" path. (What the enemy *really* means is "a more obscure and meaningless path"!) But do you honestly believe that God would ever do anything in a mediocre way or create anything or anyone without a specific purpose? Of course not! His plans are always consistent with His character.

In other words, God's plans for you are flawless and complete with nothing lacking in any area. Therefore, you need to look Satan straight in the eye and declare that you have heard from God; that you will not budge from God's plan for your life; and that you know who you are in Christ. You will *not* be moved!

Dream Thief Number Three:
Friends

If both the passage of time and the lies of Satan fail to talk you out of the dream God has sown in your heart, some of your friends will probably come forward to help you see things in a more "balanced perspective."

Many of your friends will have a confirming witness in their spirits and will know you've heard from God. They will fully support you and pray for you as you pursue your dream. But that probably won't be the case with all those who are close to you. The friends who have always known you after the flesh may expect you to think and act the way *they* have always perceived you. For the convenience and comfort of their own flesh, these friends have placed you in a pattern — *their* pattern — and they don't want you to change. Change frightens such people because their security rests in things that are temporal, not eternal.

Change isn't the only thing that frightens people who see things only from a natural perspective. If your friends think their lives are mediocre, average, or ordinary, your quest for excellence in God will probably threaten them, and they may very well try to convince you to do otherwise. I say this kindly but truthfully: Your success in obeying God will amplify any other believer's failure to faithfully pursue God's plan for his or her life.

Negativity is one of the hallmark indications that flesh is in operation. So when these friends hear about your plans, they may respond by giving you a detailed description of every disastrous scenario that could occur — even warning of catastrophes that could never happen! Flesh never believes God or His Word, and it always looks for the worst in every situation.

For instance, if God has told you to step out and start a new business, your friends might offer this advice: "Have you considered job security? You have a guaranteed salary and great benefits where you are now, so why rock the boat? How can you place your family in such jeopardy?"

I wonder how many men and women have missed the big picture for their lives by refusing to let go of the tiny part of the picture that made them feel secure?

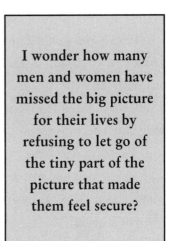

I wonder how many men and women have missed the big picture for their lives by refusing to let go of the tiny part of the picture that made them feel secure?

When someone gets saved, or when God calls a person to fulfill a specific assignment, the Holy Spirit will very often separate that person from his friends and even from his family for a while until he can begin to understand who he is in Christ and become established in that new identity. That person's life in God may take a radically different direction than the way he was heading in the past. As a result, his divine destiny may not fit neatly inside other people's expectations of "what he should do with his life."

That's why you need to be careful when you share the vision God has given to you with your friends. Be aware that some may try to keep you in the box of past patterns — the way they've always perceived you to be. As these friends talk to you about your dream, deep inside they may be thinking, *Who are you to think that you're different from us?*

During these times of testing, we must believe and obey God rather than men. Although it's true that the Holy Spirit will use the doubters and mockers to cause us to "count the cost," it's also true that pursuing God's plan for our lives may cost us some friends! But if it comes to the point where a friend turns away from us because we decide to step out and obey God, we must ask ourselves if that person is truly our friend.

True God-given friends will not only encourage you in the faith, but they will also confront you and challenge you to reexamine what God has called you to do. If they have any concerns when you share the vision God has planted in your heart, they will take the same stand the Jewish leader Gamaliel took regarding the apostles' belief that Jesus of Nazareth was the Messiah. This great teacher of the Law stood up and declared to the other members of the Sanhedrin:

> **And now I say unto you, Refrain from these men, and let them alone: for if this counsel or this work be of men, it will come to nought: but if it be of God, ye cannot overthrow it; lest haply ye be found even to fight against God.**
>
> **Acts 5:38,39**

If it becomes evident to these godly friends that God's hand is on your plans, they will support and encourage you in the cause, even if they don't totally understand it. If they do have doubts about the new direction you're about to take, they won't drag you into unbelief with their negative words and attitude. Instead, they will pray for you as they wait to receive more understanding on whether the dream you're pursuing truly originated in God. And as you press forward in fulfilling your dream, your true friends will stick with you through thick and thin, loving you through your failures as well as your successes.

> As you press forward in fulfilling your dream, your true friends will stick with you through thick and thin, loving you through your failures as well as your successes.

DREAM THIEF NUMBER FOUR: *FAMILY*

If your dream survives such challenges as the passage of time, the lies of the devil, and the opposition of friends, the final challenge is often the most difficult and painful — because it pertains to your family. Time passes and brings new seasons; the devil's voice can be rebuked and silenced; and you can tell your friends good-bye. But your family is with you for your entire life! You grow up loving your family members, and you never lose your deep desire for their love and approval.

However, sometimes it's difficult to show love and respect to your family and obey God at the same time. At times, it's like walking a tight rope, even as you continue to believe God that one day all your family members will be saved, filled with the Holy Spirit, and taking faith-filled steps toward their own divine destinies!

My own family has seen me take many leaps of faith in my life. At this point, they no longer question me when I tell them I've heard from God on a matter. But this wasn't always true.

The fact is, when any of us first begin to hear from the Lord, He may ask us to take certain radical steps in order to follow His plan for our lives. In that situation, our family members — because they love us — may very well question our judgment.

When Denise and I been married only a few years, I was the pastor of a small church, and we were so poor that my gross income for one year was a little less than $2,000! The windows in our house were all broken, so we used towels, underwear, and anything else we could find to cover the cracks in the glass.

Only one room in our house had heat, and because the kitchen had water leakage, its floor was often covered with a thin sheet of ice in the winter. And when any of our family members came to visit us, they'd always eat before they came because they knew we wouldn't have hardly any food in our home.

It was during this time that Denise and I began to dream about beginning a traveling ministry. We were young and inexperienced, but we sensed that it was time for us to get started with the dream God had put in our hearts.

When my family learned of our vision to begin a traveling ministry, they immediately converged on the scene. *"Leave your church?"* they asked me. *"Leave your house? Are you sure this is right?"* As my family members voiced doubt after doubt, I kept thinking, *It isn't like I'm giving up a whole lot here!* Even so, launching out into a traveling ministry with no guaranteed income was a great step of faith for Denise and me at the time, and it was difficult for us to handle the uncertainty voiced by our family.

This last dream thief is much more personal to you. After all, your family members watched you grow up in the natural. More than anyone else in the world, they know your faults and weaknesses. So when you announce, "The Lord told me to do this," some family members may try to explain away your dream by reminding you of your past mistakes and failures. They may try to convince you that you're compensating for your inadequacies by living in a fantasy world instead of facing your problems realistically and living life as "normal people" do.

But here's what you must always remember: All the dream thieves will come to you with an element of truth. Your mind will respond:

- *Yes, time, it has been a long while since the Holy Spirit spoke to me about my dream.*

- *Yes, Satan, I do have an ego that likes to exalt itself above others.*

- *Yes, friends, I am making major changes in my life right now, and I don't even recognize myself at times.*

- *Yes, family, I admit to the faults and weaknesses you have seen in me all my life.*

But you must face head-on the accusations and uncertainties voiced by these dream thieves. Deal with them according to the Word and the Spirit of God. As you do, not only will you persevere and hold fast to your dream, but you will also be strengthened in your inner man and become more like Jesus!

So hold fast to the vision God has placed in your heart —

- No matter how long it takes.

- No matter how many times you have to tell the devil that your selfish, egotistical old man is dead.

- No matter how many friends tell you that your plans are crazy and then forsake you.

- No matter how much it hurts when family members come against your dream because of their love and concern for you.

If you know that *God* is the One who placed the vision in your heart, this must take precedence over every other argument.

> **If you know that *God* is the One who placed the vision in your heart, this must take precedence over every other argument.**

This fact must assume the position of most importance in your life. It must be the truth you never lose sight of.

Hebrews 10:23 admonishes us to hold fast to *what God has spoken to us*, not to what our family or friends say. When we receive a word from the Lord, we are to embrace it with all our strength — to hold down that divine instruction so firmly that nothing and no one can steal it from us. We must *hold fast* to our dream with everything in our being!

It's Never Too Late

One of the saddest things Denise and I encounter as we travel in ministry is the realization that the Body of Christ is filled to overflowing with believers who at some point received a word from God but never did anything with it. These men and women were once burning with a passion to do something tremendous for God in this world. But then the dream thieves pressured them from every side — whittling away at their confidence and breaking down their resolve — until finally they let their dream slowly drain out of their hearts and minds. The exciting, adventurous, faith-filled life they had once envisioned and eagerly anticipated had been reduced to a boring, grinding routine.

Wherever we go to minister, we find people in this situation. They may have had a dream from Heaven burning in their hearts since they were very young. For example, some of them knew in their hearts that God had gifted them with the ability to make millions and to help finance the preaching of the Gospel throughout the world in order to bring in the end-time harvest that is currently taking place. Others knew they were born to establish their own businesses or ministries. But instead, so many of these Christians settled for less — and as a result, they have lived a mediocre life.

When people near the end of their lives without accomplishing what God called them to do, they often look for a scapegoat. Unfortunately, one of the most common scapegoats people use is their own children. They say, "Well, if I didn't do anything else, I raised some good kids."

It's true that raising godly, healthy, and productive children should be one of our highest priorities. However, our parental responsibilities provide no excuse for ignoring or choosing not to fulfill the call of God on our lives. The truth is, if we refuse to follow the direction of the Holy Spirit in fulfilling our divine purpose, we're not setting a godly example for our children anyway. We're only perpetuating our frustration and passing down to the next generation our failure to obey God.

Here's the bottom line: *Your sense of purpose and fulfillment and your greatest joys and adventures can only be found by following God's plan for your life.*

If you realize that you have allowed the dream thieves to steal your dream, remember this: It doesn't matter how old you are, because it is never too late to begin pursuing God's purpose and plan for your life. Consider Moses, who was 80 years old when God called him out of the wilderness to confront Pharaoh!

So remember, when you receive a word from God, you must *hold fast.* Wrap your arms of faith around that divine revelation. Hold it tight, and keep it firmly planted in your heart. In other words, sit on it! Do everything in your power to keep your God-given dream from being stolen from you — and then pursue it with all your might!

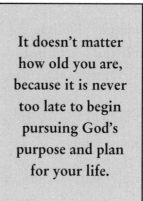

It doesn't matter how old you are, because it is never too late to begin pursuing God's purpose and plan for your life.

AN IMPORTANT NOTE

Before I proceed further, I want to say something very important. Perhaps you're reading this book and haven't yet been born again. (In other words, perhaps you haven't yet repented of your sins and declared that Jesus Christ is your personal Lord and Savior, resurrected from the dead to give you a brand-new life.) You may have some ideas about God's purpose and plan for your life because you've recognized and pursued your talents, abilities, and interests.

However, you will never know why you were created without knowing your Creator.

You will never know the best plan for your life without knowing the Designer of that plan.

And you will never know true fulfillment without knowing Jesus Christ.

Therefore, if you haven't ever repented of your sin and made Jesus your Lord and Savior, I strongly urge you to do it right now. Don't wait another second. You can begin today to discover the divine purpose behind your talents, abilities, and deep desires!

THINK ABOUT IT

Before the foundation of the world, God had a plan for your life. As He knit you together in your mother's womb, your Heavenly Father breathed dreams into your spirit aligned with that plan. Those God-given dreams reflect your special individuality, calling, and divine giftings. You are called to be conformed to the image of Jesus Christ, not to the image or opinions of your family and friends.

Do you know what qualities or aspirations you have that make you unique? Have your friends or family ever caused you to question your gifts or yourself because your talents are different from theirs? If so, what did you learn from that experience?

If you will be honest with yourself, you will find that your own desires and abilities reveal the outline of God's design for your life. In an attempt to inject fear, dream-destroying forces will attack your mind, your will, and your emotions until you retreat from what God has revealed to you. But if you will face those attacks instead of hiding from them and then answer any questions that arise in the midst of the experience, you will find the determination you need to move forward.

What is a key dream in your life? Are you certain it's from God? How do you know?

What is within your ability to do at this time to help bring your God-given dream to pass? Have you taken any of these steps yet? If not, why not?

The reason many people fail is not for lack of vision, but for lack of resolve — and resolve is born out of counting the cost. Consider what it will take to turn your dream into reality. When you consider potential obstacles *before* you actually face them, you will develop an inner resolve to endure whatever you encounter along the way.

What obstacles stand between you and your dream? What preparation is needed to help you overcome those obstacles? What changes do you need to make in your life in order to fulfill your God-given dream?

Are you willing to stop making excuses and lay aside a life of mediocrity so you can take steps toward fulfilling the vision God has given you? What do you have to lose? What do you have to gain?

CHAPTER TWO

COMING INTO DIVINE ALIGNMENT

*W*e've discussed some of the dream thieves that try to come against God's plan for your life and the importance of "holding fast" to your dream. We'll talk about a few other dream thieves later, but first I want to address a vital point. If you want to see your God-given dream fulfilled in your life, you absolutely must understand the next part of Hebrews 10:23, which says, "Let us hold fast the *profession* of our faith...."

The Greek word for "profession" is *homologia*. In its most simple translation, this word means *to say the same thing*. The first part of this word, *homo*, means *of the same kind*. It is where we derive the word "homogenus" (*of the same species*). The second part of the word, *logia*, is the Greek word *logos*, meaning *words*. When the two words are compounded together, they form the word *homologia*, which means *to say the same thing*. Some translations also render this word "confession."

However, in this verse, the word *homologia* conveys even more. When a person makes a true profession, he speaks forth words that God has sown into his heart, not just glibly repeating what he's heard someone else say.

Many Christians don't understand this principle. Sincerely trying to move into a new realm of faith, they walk around merely repeating words they heard from a preacher or a fellow believer. *Yet because their profession comes only out of their mouths and not from their hearts, their words don't produce results — no matter how convincing they may sound.* Such people need to spend time in the Word and in prayer until their profession of faith in what God has said reflects what they steadfastly believe in their own hearts.

Jesus said, "For verily I say unto you, That whosoever shall say unto this mountain, Be thou removed, and be thou cast into the sea; *and shall not doubt in his heart, but shall believe those things which he saith shall come to pass,* he shall have whatsoever he saith" (Mark 11:23).

Anyone who believes the Bible would have to honestly say that Jesus was teaching about the principles of faith and confession in this verse. There is no doubt — by Jesus' own admission — that our faith and our mouths must be *connected.* According to this verse, the key to a successful, faith-filled confession is to have no doubt in our hearts and to believe the things we say. Only when this prerequisite is met can we have "whatsoever we saith."

Several years ago, I was staying at a friend's house in Michigan. Early in the morning, the telephone began to ring, but no one was getting up to answer it. I waited and waited for someone to wake up and answer the phone until I had counted

34 telephone rings. Finally, I thought to myself, *I guess I'll get up and answer the phone, since no one else will!*

I put on my clothes in the darkness of the early morning. Then I walked downstairs, picked up the receiver, and said, "Hello" — but the telephone just kept on ringing and ringing and ringing.

Baffled and curious, I looked over to my right side and saw a huge bird cage covered with a tablecloth. When I peeked under that cloth, I realized it was a parrot making those ringing noises over and over again — and he sounded exactly like a real telephone! Yet just because that bird could make *sounds* like a telephone, it didn't mean he *was* a telephone!

Many believers act like that parrot, repeating again and again what God's Word or someone else says but with no depth of faith or understanding behind their words. They say the right things, but they do so in a mechanical way.

A mechanical confession is *not* what the Holy Spirit is referring to in Hebrews 10:23. This type of profession doesn't come from the heart and therefore doesn't bring forth any fruit.

The power of confession is real; we read what Jesus said about its power in Mark 11:23. But a true faith confession must come from your *heart* before it comes out of your *mouth*. This connection between heart and mouth is crucial if your profession is to produce a harvest of blessings in your life.

I remember back in the early days when Denise and I first began to move in the power of God and were just learning to walk in faith. I went to a meeting where people gave tremendous testimonies of their miraculous healings, and I took note of one man's testimony in particular. He said that after he had thrown his contact lenses away, he could see perfectly.

> A true faith confession must come from your *heart* before it comes out of your *mouth*.

With almost no thought — and with no understanding of what it really meant to step out in faith — I said to myself, *Well, I'm going to do what that man did!* So I removed my glasses, threw them down on the ground, and stomped them into a thousand pieces. Later I stumbled out of the meeting, my eyesight unchanged — and as I drove home, I suddenly realized I was a lethal weapon on the road!

I hadn't really acted in faith when I stomped on my glasses. I had merely copied what someone else had done.

I believe this is one of the reasons why so many Christians have been disappointed and disillusioned when they've attempted to move in the power of confession. The problem, however, doesn't lie in the power of faith or in the validity of faith-filled confessions. The problem lies with *them*. Their confessions don't come from their hearts. And because they haven't really embraced the truth of what they're saying, their confession is only mechanical — not much different than a parrot that repeats what it has heard someone else say.

The way to avoid parrot-like, mindless confessions is to first make certain you have chosen to believe what God says. You see, sometimes you can receive a word from the Lord and *instantly* have a powerful revelation of what the Holy Spirit is saying to you. However, most of the time, because the natural mind can't fathom the things of God's Spirit (1 Corinthians 2:14), you'll have to pick up your Bible and do some prayerful, serious study and meditation. Commit yourself with all your heart and strength to standing in faith on the Word of God, no matter how crazy it may sound to your natural mind. Then *meditate* on the scriptures the Holy Spirit quickens to your spirit. Ask Him to make the Word more real and rock solid to you than the natural things that surround you. This is the way you come to a stance of faith in which you truly understand and confess *from your heart* what God is saying to you.

MORE THAN A WORD

The key to what makes one's profession more than just the parroting of someone else's words can be found in the word *logia*, the second half of the word "profession" (*homologia*). This word comes from the word *logos*, which, as mentioned earlier, is the Greek word for *words*. But *logos* means more than just words; it also refers to *the concept, opinion, emotion, or reasoning behind the words being communicated.*

For example, when you read one of my books, you're not just reading words — you're reading *my* words. You can't divorce my words on the printed page from my life because my words convey my convictions, my beliefs, and my passions. And if you confess or profess the words I have written, you are agreeing with or coming into alignment with *me*.

Likewise, when we talk about professing or confessing *God's Word*, we are actually saying that we're coming into alignment with *God*. I call this *divine alignment*. The word "profession" or "confession" (*homologia*) not only means *to say it like God says it*, but, more specifically, it means *to see it like God sees it, to feel it like God feels it*, and *to know it like God knows it* — until our hearts finally begin to beat in sync with His very heart.

Logos is a very powerful word! When you read God's *logos*, you are reading His heart, His mind, His ways, His plans, and His purposes. Therefore, if you hold fast to the *profession* of your faith by saying the same words as God's Word, you are choosing to align your life with His life. You are causing your will to line up with His will. You are determining to shove aside all preconceived notions about your calling — all of your desires and self-made plans — in order to come into alignment with God's plan for your life. You are choosing to become one with your divine purpose.

> If you hold fast to the *profession* of your faith by saying the same words as God's Word, you are choosing to align your life with His life.

ARE YOU ALIGNED WITH GOD'S PURPOSES?

One of the main reasons Christians never see their dream or vision realized is that they never come to this place of divine alignment, where they begin to *say* the same thing God says and *do it* the way God wants it done. Again, God insists on this because He wants to bring forth Christ-likeness in the lives of His people.

As you align yourself with God, you become more like Him. His plan is not just to bless you, nor does He want you to do it His way just to prove your obedience to Him. He wants to *transform* you from the inside out and make you into the image of Jesus Christ.

When you receive a word from the Lord, you find out very quickly whether or not you're walking in divine alignment. God probably intended for Sarah and Abraham to celebrate the birth of their baby nine months after receiving the word from Heaven that they were going to have a child. But because Abraham was totally out of alignment, it took him several decades to receive the promised child, Isaac.

For years after receiving the promise of a son, Abraham tried to figure everything out on his own instead of waiting on the Lord's perfect plan. God could do nothing to bring the promise to pass until Abraham finally decided to leave everything in the Lord's hands and do it *His* way (in other words, until Abraham finally came into divine alignment).

We find out just how aligned we are with God when we receive a word from Him telling us to do something different than we're used to. For example, when the Holy Spirit directed me to move my family to the Soviet Union and help establish churches in the great revival that was taking place there, my first reaction was *not*, "Yes, Lord, send me!" In fact, I cried out in pain, "But what about our ministry in America, Lord?"

Denise and I had spent the previous six years traveling across the United States, working hard as we strove to accomplish what God had called us to do, and everything was finally beginning to fall into place. Major ministers were starting to recognize our teaching ministry and were recommending my books. We had to turn down meeting after meeting as we prayerfully arranged our schedule. And, most importantly, people were being saved, healed, delivered, and strengthened through our ministry.

Now it seemed like God was asking us to give up all that had been accomplished. Just when all the seed we had sown through the years was finally producing a rich harvest, I thought that God was telling us to give the farm away! But there was no mistaking God's direction to us. To be honest, it was a great struggle for me to come to a place of surrender and obedience regarding God's call on our lives to minister in the Soviet Union. And as I wrestled with the decision to obey, I found out just how "out of divine alignment" I was!

First, I tried to buy off God. I told Him that I'd send the missionaries in the Soviet Union all the teaching tapes they wanted. Not only that, I promised, but I would also give as much financial support to their ministries and to other missionaries in the world as the Lord directed me to give.

Still, God's word to me remained unchanged: *Move to the Soviet Union.*

When my first tactic didn't seem to satisfy God, I agreed to make a trip to Russia with some other evangelists, hoping that the visit would appease God and relieve me of this terrible burden in my heart. Instead, the trip served to drive the "Holy Spirit hook" deeper into my heart, for I fell in love with the Russian people.

Finally, I thought my deliverance would surely come when I told my wife that God was telling me that we were supposed to move to the Soviet Union. Instead of bursting into tears and strongly arguing against the idea of making such a drastic move, Denise tearfully and joyfully *agreed* that this was God's plan and we had to obey.

There was no way around it now! If we were going to obey God and walk in divine alignment with His plan and purpose for our lives, we would have to move to the USSR.

So I made the official announcement, taking great pleasure in boldly proclaiming the word of the Lord for our lives. Then this great man of faith went home and hung his head over a toilet bowl for 24 hours, waiting for the next vomiting spell! Anxiety flowed through my veins; worry filled my mind; and nothing I did helped to relax me.

All I could think about was the prospect of my family going broke and losing our home in the United States. I worried about the ministry going down the tubes and our staff members not being able to feed and clothe their families. Money, money, *money*! How would we ever manage?

When I finally received and acted on this word from the Lord, everything in me that wasn't in alignment with God's will came rushing to the surface, along with every ounce of doubt and unbelief still residing in my soul. All I could think about was *money*! Over and over I cried out in my heart, *Lord, what will happen to our ministry if I obey You?* Finally, I not only heard the Holy Spirit's answer, but I also began to understand what He was trying to tell me. He spoke these words to my heart: "*What will you MISS if you don't obey Me?"* That question brought me to a new place of surrender in my walk with God.

PLIABLE IN THE HANDS OF GOD

Nothing is more thrilling than those times when the Holy Spirit moves supernaturally to give you a grand and glorious plan to follow. However, there's always the pound of flesh that has to be cut off in order for you to come into divine alignment, enter into God's supernatural rest, and carry out His will for your life.

What if you received a word from the Lord right now to quit a company where you'd been employed for ten years in order to start a new business? The idea may seem exciting in the beginning as you envision great sums of money pouring into your office that you can then funnel into the preaching of the Gospel. But as you begin to consider all that your obedience requires of you personally, your flesh won't be so enthralled!

I am reminded of the man who had lain at the pool of Bethesda his entire life (John 5:1-9). Think of all his friends who were there, waiting for an angel to stir the waters along with him. If the man ever did get healed, he'd have to leave those friends. He'd also have to stop depending on others and get a job! His entire lifestyle would be drastically changed.

Therefore, it was very significant when Jesus asked this paralyzed man, "...Wilt thou be made whole?" (John 5:6). In essence, Jesus was asking him, "Do you want to be healed, and do you understand the sweeping ramifications of this supernatural work in your life?"

It's much easier to give up everything to obey God when you don't have very much. Such was the case for Denise and me when He called us into the traveling ministry so many years ago. We didn't have anything we were leaving behind, so it was easy to say yes to our next season of ministry. But it can be much more difficult when God has enabled you to build something great and wonderful, and then He asks you to lay it all down and move on to a new work that is yet unformed!

The most thrilling aspect of choosing to obey God's will for your life and coming into divine alignment, however, is knowing that you're still pliable enough in His hands to give up everything you have if He requires it of you. *After God has made you "ruler over much," your greatest joy and reward lies in the realization that you are still, above all else, His faithful servant.*

> The most thrilling aspect of choosing to obey God's will for your life and coming into divine alignment is knowing that you're still pliable enough in His hands to give up everything you have if He requires it of you.

All those who want to fully follow God's plan for their lives must come to this realization deep down in their hearts. It is only from this position of solid, unequivocal alignment with God's will that they can move forward to fulfill their divine destiny in total confidence and unshakable faith.

Think About It

Amos 3:3 states, "Can two walk together, except they be agreed?" In order to come into alignment with God, you must agree with Him in your heart — not merely with your words. Simply parroting a principle without believing it from the heart is not agreement. Life-directing confessions of power are those that come from the heart, springing forth from a deeply held belief.

What do you really believe about your God-given vision and dream?

By choosing to align your thoughts, words, and actions with God's words, you bring your will into alignment with His plan for your life. As a result, you become unified with your own divine purpose.

What area of your character are you consciously working on right now to bring into alignment with God's will and His ways? What areas have you been ignoring?

Are you pliable in God's hands? Are you willing to conform to God, or are you trying to make God conform to you? Be honest. What are you willing to change in your life in order to fulfill your divine destiny?

Pruning is part of the process to become fruitful. There are some things that must be trimmed back or cut off in order for you to come in line with God's supernatural plan for your life.

What are the areas in your life in need of pruning? God's plan may require you to lay aside something you want so you can obtain what you desire even more. But you must first be willing to trust God and let go. What are you holding on to that may actually be hindering you from obtaining what you want the most in life?

Your obedience — or your disobedience — to God's plan will have a direct effect on the lives of others. Have you considered how you will give account to God for what you have or have not done with the dreams, abilities, and divine giftings He has invested into your life? Contemplate the consequences of your current pursuits, and determine what you need to do differently.

CHAPTER THREE

THE BEHAVIOR OF REAL FAITH

*L*et's go back to that first phrase in Hebrews 10:23, where it says, "Let us hold fast the profession of our faith...." In the *King James Version*, the word "our" is italicized, which means it doesn't actually appear in the original language. Thus, we should translate this phrase, "Let us hold fast the profession *of faith*...."

We are to tightly hold in our hearts and come into divine alignment with the word God has spoken to us. This word, whether it is a direct quote from the written Word of God or a very specific word that He has spoken to us regarding our lives, will always be a word of faith.

The Bible speaks to us most strongly about faith in Hebrews 11:1: "Now faith is the substance of things hoped for, the evidence of things not seen." Although some may say that Hebrews 11:1 is a *definition* of faith, I see this as a description of the *behavior* of faith.

DEVELOP 'BULLDOG FAITH'

I especially want you to notice the word "substance" in this verse. This is the Greek word *hupostasis*, which is another compound word. The first part of the word is *hupo*, which means *alongside*. The second part of the word is *stasis*, which means *to stand*. When compounded together, the new word means *to stand by or alongside something*.

This tells us something extremely important about faith: *When faith finally finds what it needs or wants, it never moves until it GETS what it seeks.* Or you could say that faith is like a bulldog that has finally found the bone of its wildest dreams. Once the bulldog wraps its jowls around that bone, *no one* is going to pull the bone out of its mouth! Someone may tug, pull, and try to jerk that bone out of the bulldog's mouth, but it will *not* let go. The bulldog is going to "stand by" that bone and *never* relinquish it.

> **When faith finally finds what it needs or wants, it never moves until it *gets* what it seeks.**

By understanding this meaning of *hupostasis* ("substance"), we know that this kind of faith is *determined, committed,* and *unrelenting.* It knows what it wants, and it won't let go until it gets it! This is a resolute, steadfast, full-of-grit kind of faith that has gumption and backbone. It looks straight into the face of opposition and refuses to move. It is firm, unhesitating, unflinching, indomitable, tireless, obstinate, and inflexible.

This kind of faith knows exactly what it wants. It is a faith that will not bend under pressure and has resolved to believe at any cost — rain or shine, sink or swim — until it sees the manifestation of what God has said or promised. This is the behavior of *bulldog faith* as it is described in Hebrews 11:1. You could therefore translate the verse, *"Now faith is tirelessly and determinedly standing by and never letting go of things hoped for...."*

You may ask, "Where do I get that kind of faith?" *Such faith is the overflow of a divine relationship with God that develops as you hear a word from Him and wholeheartedly commit yourself to stand by that word until you see it fulfilled in your life.* As you come into this divine alignment, faith rises up from your heart and floods your soul, providing you with the supernatural ability, tenacity, stubbornness of will, and holy boldness to stand by the dream or the vision that God has imparted to you.

It is in this state of oneness with God that we become as tenacious about the dream He has planted in our hearts as a bulldog is about its bone. It doesn't matter how long it takes, how many obstacles must be overcome, or how hard someone or something is trying to wrest that dream from our hearts or convince us that it isn't ours to fulfill. We have heard from God, and no matter what it costs us, we're not letting go of our dream! This is the behavior of true faith.

Too often I encounter people who try to make the teachings on faith sound too deep and complicated — and, as a result, no one is quite sure what the message really is! But the truth is, living by faith is very simple to understand.

The behavior of faith is demonstrated by a tenacious, unrelenting decision to stand by a word from God and refuse to let go until you see it totally fulfilled. Nothing else will do, nor will anything else satisfy if you are truly walking by faith!

The Hall of Faith

In Hebrews 11:2, the Holy Spirit continues to describe the behavior of faith: "For by it [that is, by this tenacious, committed, unrelenting faith that knows what it wants and won't give up until it receives its answer] the elders obtained a good report.

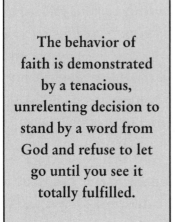

The behavior of faith is demonstrated by a tenacious, unrelenting decision to stand by a word from God and refuse to let go until you see it totally fulfilled.

Particularly notice the word "elders." According to this verse, Hebrews 11 is not really a chapter about faith itself, but about examples of Old Testament elders, both patriarchs and matriarchs, who walked by faith. The verses that follow are commonly known as "The Hall of Faith." This passage of Scripture describes the great exploits these men and women of God accomplished with their faith during the course of their lives.

Verse 3 goes on to say, "Through faith [that is, through this same kind of committed, never-give-up kind of faith] we understand that the worlds were framed by the word of God, so that things which are seen were not made of things which do appear."

At first glance, this verse seems to be talking about how God created the earth and universe. However, this would contradict verse 2, which just told us that this entire chapter is about the exploits of *Old Testament elders* and says nothing about God or creation. Moreover, the rest of the chapter outlines the exploits of Old Testament saints and says nothing about God's act of creation. If this chapter is really about the actions and the behavior of men and women who walked by faith (as verse 2 so clearly states), why would the writer of Hebrews suddenly break the flow of this message and switch to a different subject altogether by talking about the work of God in creation?

A deeper look at Hebrews 11:3 fully answers this question and reveals that this verse is actually a continuation of the previous verse. The Holy Spirit is still talking about the Old Testament patriarchs and matriarchs — those men and women of God who:

- Walked in "bulldog faith."

- Came into divine alignment with God's plan and purpose for their lives.

- Never gave up or let go of their word from God until they saw it fulfilled in their lives and for their generation.

Notice verse 3 says, "Through faith we understand that the worlds were framed by the word of God...." I want you to particularly notice the words "worlds" and "framed." By studying these two words, a fresh, new understanding of this verse emerges.

The word "worlds" comes from the Greek word *aionos*, which refers to *specific allotted periods of time within the past history of mankind, such as decades, generations, centuries, or millenniums*. All of these could be technically described as an *aionos* because each is a specific allotted period of time within the past history of mankind.

Verse 3 could thus be translated, *"Through faith we understand that different time periods — different decades, centuries, millenniums, and generations within the past history of mankind — have been framed by the word of God...."*

Now notice the word "framed." It comes from the Greek word *katartidzo*, which means *to change or alter the outward form and shape of an already existing thing.* Therefore, the Holy Spirit cannot be talking about the original creation of the world. Had He been speaking of creation, He wouldn't have used this word "framed," because this word emphatically describes *not* the creation of something new, but rather the re-creating, reshaping, remolding, and altering of something that is already in existence.

This word "framed" is the same Greek word we would use to describe what a potter does while working with a piece of clay. If he decides to change, remold, and reshape his already-existing work, he completely alters and transforms that clay into a brand-new shape. It is the same piece of clay, but now it looks different. It has a new form, a new shape, and a new look.

Therefore, the word "framed" in Hebrews 11:3 describes the *remolding, altering,* and *reshaping* of a world that already exists, not the original creation of the world that we read about in Genesis chapter 1. This dramatically changes the meaning of Hebrews 11:3. This verse isn't about the act of *creation*; it is about the act of *transformation.*

With all this in mind, the verse could more properly be translated, *"Through faith we understand that different time periods — different decades, centuries, millenniums, and generations within the past history of mankind — have been completely and radically altered, remolded, and reshaped by the word of God...."*

Now I want you to notice the phrase "by the word of God." According to the original Greek, this phrase would be better rendered, "by *a* word from God." The term "word" here is *not* the Greek word *logos*. Rather, it's taken from the Greek word *rhema*, which describes *something that is spoken clearly and vividly, in unmistakable terms and in undeniable language.* In the New Testament, the word *rhema* carries the idea of a *quickened word*. It refers to those times when the Holy Spirit speaks to a person's heart, giving him or her a specific word for a specific time and a specific purpose.

Thus, the first part of verse 3 could be translated, *"Through faith we understand that different time periods — different decades, centuries, millenniums, and generations within the past history of mankind — have been completely and radically altered, remolded, and reshaped by those who received a clear and undeniable word from God for a specific purpose...."*

Of course! This makes sense! This entire chapter is about people who received a word from God and obeyed it, no matter what the cost. Despite others' words of discouragement, despite opposition, and despite the odds that were against them, these godly men and women *knew* they had received a word from God, and they held on to that word with bulldog faith. They refused to let go of what God had promised them until they saw the promise fulfilled just as He had spoken.

Because of their bulldog tenacity, these men and women changed history! Their faith and obedience to the *rhema* word they had received caused the time periods in which they lived — their decade, their generation, their century, perhaps even their millennium — to be completely and radically changed into something brand new!

For instance, Noah received a word from God about a flood that was going to destroy the world of his day. Noah's word from God wasn't a lengthy word. It was short, concise, and to the point. Furthermore, there is no biblical record that Noah ever received a word from God before or after he received this word. As far as we know, this may have been the only specific word from Heaven Noah ever received.

God didn't give Noah 50 pages of instructions; He just gave His man a very simple directive: "Build a big boat because a flood is coming. Collect two animals of every kind, and get ready for the ride of your life!" (*see* Genesis 6:13-22).

We'll take a closer look at Noah later, but for now I want to point out his response to what God said to him. Noah knew he had heard from God, and he believed what God told him. So Noah committed himself wholeheartedly to obey the word he had received from the Lord. He determined in his heart to stand by that word from Heaven, regardless of any opposition, accusations, or slander he encountered — *and he refused to ever give in or give up*. As a result, this one man completely altered, remolded, and reshaped the history of mankind because he stood by a word from God in his generation!

How about Moses? When Moses encountered God in the burning bush on the back side of Mount Horeb, he, too, received a word from God. As in the case of Noah, the word Moses received wasn't a lengthy word. It was simple, short, concise, and straight to the point! God told Moses, "I want you to go see Pharaoh and tell him to let My people go!" (*see* Exodus 3:2-10).

Moses shuddered to think of returning to Egypt after so many years. He even argued with the Lord, saying, "...O my Lord, I am not eloquent...but I am slow of speech, and of a slow tongue" (Exodus 4:10). In essence, Moses was saying, "But, Lord, that's too big of a job! I really think You'd do well to pick another man!"

Nevertheless, when the conversation between Moses and God concluded, Moses knew he had heard a word from God. And when that divine word took root in Moses' heart, faith rose up in his heart to do what God had commanded. Against all odds — against persecution, against opposition, against the very forces of hell itself — Moses came into divine alignment with his word from Heaven and moved into the realm of bulldog faith!

Whether or not Moses ever did another thing right in his entire life, he knew he had to do this task right. He had heard from God — and regardless of the risk or the price to be paid, he was going to give it his all! Come hell or high water, Moses wholeheartedly committed himself to believe, to obey, and to hold on to that divine word until he saw it fulfilled.

Because this one man stood by a word from God in his time and in his generation, his obedience permanently altered the course of history — even toppling the ancient Egyptian empire's hold upon the world of his day! (Later we'll go into more detail about Moses as well.)

Hebrews chapter 11 goes on to name other men and women who during the course of their lives received a word from God.

> Against all odds —
> against persecution,
> against opposition,
> against the very
> forces of hell itself —
> Moses came into
> divine alignment
> with his word from
> Heaven and moved
> into the realm of
> bulldog faith!

We magnify these individuals in our minds and think of them as being super-special, almost superhuman people. But they were just normal, regular human beings, people like you and me — that is, until they each received a word from God and determined to obey it. From that moment on, it was their bulldog tenacity and their unrelenting, never-give-up brand of faith that earned them a place in the Hebrews 11 "Hall of Faith."

If these men and women had never acted on the word they received from God, we'd know nothing of them today. But they became champions of faith because of their obstinate, inflexible decision to stand by their word from God with a do-or-die, hold-on-and-never-let-go, no-nonsense kind of faith that refused to relent.

In Hebrews 11:32-34, the writer of Hebrews adds more names to "The Hall of Faith."

> **And what shall I more say? For the time would fail me to tell of Gideon, and of Barak, and of Samson, and of Jephthah; of David also, and Samuel, and of the prophets: who through faith subdued kingdoms, wrought righteousness, obtained promises,**

stopped the mouths of lions, quenched the violence of fire, escaped the edge of the sword, out of weakness were made strong, waxed valiant in fight, turned to flight the armies of the aliens....

The Bible is full of people, no different than you or I, who heard a word from God, responded in faith, came into divine alignment with what God said, and ultimately saw His word to them fulfilled in their lives. And because of these people's commitment to believe and to possess what God had promised, they changed history!

The same should be true in your life. If God speaks a word to your heart and tells you to start a business, then start a business! If He calls you to the ministry, then do everything you can do to prepare to answer that call. Don't wait for someone to give you a 50-page prophecy before you obey the word from God you have already heard!

God rarely speaks to us in such a lengthy manner because He knows we're too simple to comprehend a long, detailed word. Remember God's simple message to Noah: "Build a boat!" His word to Moses was also simple: "Tell Pharaoh to let My people go!" God will speak to us on our level in a way we can understand — and He will usually be straight to the point!

Occasionally people come to Denise and me and ask us to read prophecies they have received for their lives. Some of the prophecies we've read are 10 to 20 pages in length, yet they usually contain one basic message: "Do this. Do that. Obey Me in this matter, and see what I will do!"

Of course, God certainly has the right and the option to speak to a person in a lengthy prophetic word. However, many times when we read a long prophecy, it is evident that the person probably heard a short, simple word from God but then attempted to dress it up in more "spiritual terms" to make it sound more profound and significant in the eyes of others.

When it comes to following God's will for your life, don't try to be so complicated! The truth is, it will take every ounce of your strength and determination to come into alignment with even a so-called *small* word from Heaven. But as you believe what God has said with all your heart and do exactly what He has instructed you to do, you will experience the same results that Noah and Moses did. You will witness God's power in operation to dramatically *alter*, *remold*, and *reshape* your family, your church, your business, your city, your nation, and even your generation to the glory of God!

> **It will take every ounce of your strength and determination to come into alignment with even a so-called *small* word from Heaven.**

Digging In Your Heels

You may ask, "But what about the odds that are against me? What about the opposition I'm facing?"

Let me ask you this:

- How badly do you want to see God move in your life?

- How badly do you want to see that word from Heaven fulfilled?

- Do you want to stay where you are right now — or do you want to change?

- Do you want to accomplish and fulfill the dream God has planted in your heart — or are you willing to live your entire life in stagnation, knowing that you never did what God called you to do?

- How would you like to actually do what others have only dreamed of doing?

You see, the choice is yours to make. If you really want to see your God-given dream come to pass, you must embrace and pursue it with all your heart and with bulldog faith. Absolutely *nothing* else will do!

To review, let's go back to the expanded translation of Hebrews 11:3:

> *"Through faith we understand that different time periods — different decades, centuries, millenniums, and generations within the past history of mankind — have been completely and radically altered, remolded, and reshaped by those who received a clear and undeniable word from God for a specific purpose...."*

In fact, the reshaping of these different time periods was so complete that the verse goes on to say, "...so that things which are seen were not made of things which do appear." The idea being expressed here is this: *By the time these men and women were finished obeying God, their generation was so thoroughly changed that the world didn't look anything like it did when they first began to believe and obey God.*

For instance, consider again the lives of Noah and Moses. By the time the obedience of each of these elders had been fulfilled, the world of their day had been completely restructured. The situation that existed after their obedience looked totally different than it did before they stepped out and obeyed God. Yet prior to their obedience, no one would have believed that such a radical reshaping of events was possible!

> **Throughout the Word of God, this truth is demonstrated in the lives of godly men and women: Standing by one word from the Lord can change an entire generation!**

Throughout the Word of God, this truth is demonstrated in the lives of godly men and women: Standing by one word from the Lord can change an entire generation!

NOAH:
PAYING THE PRICE

Like all of us, Noah wasn't perfect; in fact, he made some big mistakes in his life. But when he received a divine communication from God, Noah stood by that word. The Lord told him, "Noah, I'm going to flood the earth, so I want you to build a boat. Put a male and a female of every species on the boat, and when I give the signal, climb aboard. I'll shut the door Myself.

Then when the time is right, I'll let you out, along with all the other creatures."

This wasn't a particularly intricate or lengthy word; yet I'm certain that the dream thieves tried every trick they knew in order to keep Noah from building that boat. First of all, we know that Noah surely had to deal with dream thief number one, *time*. The Bible says that from the time Noah received this word from God until it came to pass was a span of many years.

Decade after decade, Noah preached one message — the word he had received from God. Meanwhile, he came into divine alignment with that word by building a boat and collecting animals. Satan — dream thief number two — no doubt reminded Noah on numerous occasions that it had never rained on the earth before and that what he was preaching was completely ludicrous to even consider.

You see, until the time of the Flood, the earth had been surrounded by a canopy of mist. The whole planet was like one huge greenhouse in which the land was watered by the dew every morning. The skies had never dropped rain, nor had the bowels of the earth released water. Man had never seen or even heard of a "flood."

We also know from the biblical account that all of Noah's friends and most of his family forsook him because only members of his immediate family got on the boat. Therefore, it stands to reason that many family members were probably quick to tell Noah that he shouldn't be so fanatical. More than likely, they kept complaining and accusing him of being an embarrassment to them right up to the time the rain began to fall.

In addition, we can only imagine the ridicule this man of God endured as he collected animals from all over the earth! Just think of what people must have thought as Noah began gathering two of every species in his backyard — lions, tigers, bears, and so forth — because God was about to do something no one had ever seen before.

Have we ever truly pondered the ramifications of Noah's obedience? The very fact that Noah succeeded in fulfilling this one simple word from God for his life indicates that he held on to what God had said with awesome tenacity and resolve. Noah *truly* held fast to his profession of faith! And because he counted the cost and chose to pay the price, Noah's obedience upheld God's purposes on the earth and affected *all* the generations that were yet to be born.

> Because he counted the cost and chose to pay the price, Noah's obedience upheld God's purposes on the earth and affected *all* the generations that were yet to be born.

MOSES:
A MAN OF DESTINY

Because Pharaoh feared the growing numbers of the children of Israel, he ordered all male Hebrew babies to be killed at birth. But when Moses was born, his mother defied the Pharaoh's edict and hid her baby for three months. Then she put him in a waterproof basket and hid him in the reeds on the bank of the Nile River (*see* Exodus 1:22-2:10).

In her desire to spare her child's life, this mother succeeded in preserving God's purposes. In His sovereignty, God placed that little basket in the hands of Pharaoh's daughter, who came down to the river to take her bath at that moment.

It was very significant and no coincidence that Pharaoh's daughter found Moses in the great Nile River. You see, the religion of the Egyptians taught them that the Nile River was the birthplace of their gods and that the Nile was the great mother of all the gods. God purposely placed the child in the Nile, knowing that when Pharaoh's daughter found him there, she would immediately perceive that the baby was a gift of the Nile, the newest god given to Egypt. Thus, she named him Moses, which means *one drawn from the water* — a name that would indicate to all that this child had been given by the gods.

This belief generated remarkable favor for young Moses. The child was adopted by Pharaoh's daughter and trained to become the next ruler of Egypt. The First-Century Jewish historian Josephus records that, as heir to the throne, Moses was placed in charge of the Egyptian armies and succeeded in conquering the Ethiopians.[1] Moses was also considered a great orator, mathematician, and educator.

But one day a strange thing happened to this man whom Egypt was grooming to be its next pharaoh. As Moses was inspecting the work of the Hebrew slaves, he saw an Egyptian overseer brutally beating one of them.

This should have had no impact on Moses, who by now had seen his share of violence on the battlefield. Nor should he have

[1] Josephus: Book II, Chapter 10, Paragraphs 1,2.

felt any kind of pity or compassion for the Hebrew people, for he had been raised as a pagan Egyptian.

It seems that Moses had little knowledge of the Hebrews or their ways; yet as he watched this Hebrew slave being beaten, a sudden, uncontrollable rage burst forth from deep inside him, propelling him forward with a silent scream: *I must deliver this Hebrew!* Without hesitation, Moses slew the Egyptian and quickly buried him in the sand.

Later when news of his crime reached the Egyptian court, Moses fled for his life and disappeared into the wilderness. By divine "coincidence," he just happened to stop at the well of a distant relative named Jethro.

When Moses arrived at the well, Jethro's seven daughters were being harassed by wild herdsmen. Again Moses experienced an inexplicable urge to deliver these strangers from harm. He had never met these young women and didn't even realize he was related to them; yet everything in Moses' being cried out, *I must deliver these Hebrews!* (*See* Exodus 2:15-17.)

This was the call of God awakening in Moses' life. For the first time, he was sensing the inner stirrings of a word from Heaven specifically for him: *"Let My people go!"* It was a divine word destined to shake nations and change the course of history.

Born under the sentence of death, Moses' young life was miraculously spared and supernaturally directed by God to bring

Moses into divine alignment with His plan and purpose for his life. As Moses tended Jethro's sheep in the wilderness for the next 40 years, God put the finishing touches on the man He had chosen to be Israel's deliverer and one of the greatest prophets who ever lived.

> Moses sensed the inner stirrings of a word from Heaven specifically for him: *"Let My people go!"* It was a divine word destined to shake nations and change the course of history.

Finally, Moses encountered God Almighty in the burning bush and heard God's command loud and clear: "Come now therefore, and I will send thee unto Pharaoh, that thou mayest bring forth my people the children of Israel out of Egypt" (Exodus 3:10).

Just like all of us, Moses didn't feel capable of fulfilling the word he had just received. He responded to the Lord, "...*Who am I,* that I should go unto Pharaoh, and that I should bring forth the children of Israel out of Egypt?" (Exodus 3:11). At that moment, Moses was listening to the dream thieves!

No doubt, Moses' mind was rehearsing over and over again all his faults and past failures. But he still didn't realize one crucial truth: Through all Moses' downfalls and despite all his shortcomings, God had been molding and preparing him to carry out His will — to deliver the children of Israel out of the bondage of slavery in Egypt.

Later after God supernaturally confirmed to Moses that He would always be with him, guiding and protecting him, Moses tenaciously and wholeheartedly took hold of this word from the

Lord and did not rest until it was fulfilled. Moses' decision to embrace the word he had received from Heaven opened the way for God to mightily use him. Not only did Moses deliver the Hebrews out of Egypt, but he also wrote the first five books of the Bible and performed some of the most spectacular miracles recorded in the Word of God!

When we receive a word from God for our lives, it's important for us to remember that the Holy Spirit will use whatever we have been or have done in the past to equip us for success in fulfilling the vision He has given us. Romans 8:28 says it well: "And we know that all things work together for good to them that love God, to them who are the called according to his purpose."

> When we receive a word from God for our lives, it's important for us to remember that the Holy Spirit will use whatever we have been or have done in the past to equip us for success in fulfilling the vision He has given us.

MARY:
AN UNLIKELY CHOICE

Have you ever wondered why God chose Mary to bear the Son of God? She was not the most likely candidate from a natural standpoint. Mary was very young, between 12 and 14 years of age; she was from a very poor family; and she was uneducated.

As a female, Mary wasn't allowed to hear the Word of God in the synagogue, discuss theology, or receive any of the spiritual teaching available to women today. These activities were strictly forbidden to women under Jewish law. According to the law, Mary was destined to stay at home, get married, have children, and remain ignorant of spiritual matters.

So why did God choose Mary? To help us answer that question, let's look at Mary's response when Gabriel appeared to her and announced that she had been chosen to bear the Messiah (see Luke 1:26-33). Mary asked the angel, "...How shall this be, seeing I know not a man?" (Luke 1:34).

Mary wasn't rejecting the word of the Lord; she simply wanted to know how that word was going to come to pass. Obviously, questions were racing through her mind. Mary didn't know anything about theology; she didn't even know who this awesome creature was as he stood there telling her all these incredible things. She only knew, as did all Jews, that one day Someone called the Messiah would come and do great and wonderful things for her people. But now this glorious being was standing before her, declaring that *she* was the one who would bring forth "the Son of the Highest" into the world (Luke 1:32)!

It hits you when you really think about it. Considering the limited amount of knowledge of God's Word that Mary possessed, it's astounding that she didn't pass out or flee for her very life when Gabriel appeared to her! It's even more astonishing that she made the decision to quietly accept what the angel said to her.

But God knew Mary's heart — that she would ask questions and ponder the answers in her heart for the rest of her life. He

> Mary was chosen because God knew she would commit herself to a word from Him and never go back on her decision, no matter what it cost her personally.

knew that ultimately she would choose, in total submission to His will, to allow Him to use her. Thus, Mary was chosen because God knew she would commit herself to a word from Him and never go back on her decision, no matter what it cost her personally.

When Mary received her word from God and responded, "...Be it unto me according to thy word..." (Luke 1:38), everything in her instantly came into divine alignment. Through her simple act of believing, obeying, and standing by one simple word from God, this one woman changed all of history!

ARE YOU IN THE HALL OF FAITH?

My friend, God has had His hand on your life since before the foundation of the world. He has patiently and tenderly watched you through conception, covered you in the womb, separated you from your mother's womb, and predestined you to step into His divine plan for your life.

Perhaps you'd say, "I haven't heard a clear word of direction from God yet" or "I haven't experienced deep longings and desires about my divine purpose on this earth or imagined great things for my life." If that is true for you, I encourage you to get into God's Word and seek the guidance of the Holy Spirit. When you hear one simple word from the Lord and choose to stand by that word no matter what, the grace and power that God then floods into your life is truly a life-changing experience. So don't let this opportunity pass you by!

You cease to be a *history student* when you determine to hold fast to even just one word from God for your life — putting away all fear, doubt, and unbelief as you come into divine alignment with Him. From that point on, you begin the fabulous and breathtaking adventure of becoming a *history maker*!

Think About It

Real faith stands by a word from God with tireless determination. It reveals "bulldog tenacity," refusing to let go of that which has been promised. This kind of faith is the overflow of a vital relationship with God. It develops as you commit yourself fully to standing by His promise for your life until you see it come to pass.

Are you lacking tireless determination? Do you need to reinforce your intimate connection with God and His Word?

God's word to you is simple, not complicated. As you choose to believe and to act upon it — regardless of the discouraging words you may hear from the dream thieves — the divine root of faith will spring up in you.

Write down the things you know that God has spoken to your heart about your life. What are some of the ways He has been preparing you to walk in the fulfillment of His plans for you?

Take some time to consider the stories of the men and women in Scripture who made the commitment to believe and obey God, regardless of any challenge or circumstance they might face. When you move into the realm of bulldog faith, you can stand steady against all odds to see your divinely inspired dream come to pass.

What is the price you must pay to fulfill the dream God has given you? Are you willing to pay that price? If not, are you willing to allow God to help you *become* willing?

God takes pleasure in selecting unlikely people for unusual tasks. He has a distinct plan for your life that He will make clear as you seek Him through His Word. Your faith-filled response to God's Word will not only alter your life — it will change history. Remember: Your dream is not just for you.

What dreams do you hold that, when fulfilled, will make a difference in the lives of others?

CHAPTER FOUR

SUSTAINING YOUR FIRE FOR THE DREAM IN YOUR HEART

*A*ll those who are born into God's Kingdom by accepting Jesus Christ as their Lord and Savior receive a specific purpose for their lives — and you are no exception. You were born again by the Spirit of God not only to be a child of God, but to be a child of God with *power*! As John 1:12 so clearly states, "But as many as received him [Jesus], to them gave he *power* to become the sons of God, even to them that believe on his name."

You have the power of God! That divine power is resident within you by virtue of your new nature. It came at the very moment of the new birth, when the Holy Spirit first regenerated your dead human spirit and made it alive unto God.

At that precise moment, all the power of Heaven came down to recreate the part of you that was dead — the part of you that had never known God nor expressed itself in godly terms. Instantly your spirit was utterly changed. In that split second of time, you passed from the realm of death into life (1 John 3:14) as

God rescued you out of the kingdom of darkness and translated you into the Kingdom of His dear Son (Colossians 1:13).

Suddenly all of God's plans for your life — plans that were set in motion even before the foundation of the world — began to burst forth and blossom before your very eyes. Your purpose, your destiny, your reason for living (for your life is by no means accidental!) began to come into clearer focus.

That's why the main goal of all believers should be to find God's plan for their lives and then to pursue it with all their might and strength — and that includes you and me. Doing God's will and fulfilling the purpose for which we were born must be our greatest desire and our highest aspiration in life.

> The main goal of all believers should be to find God's plan for their lives and then to pursue it with all their might and strength — and that includes you and me.

God told Jeremiah, "Before I formed thee in the belly I knew thee; and before thou camest forth out of the womb I sanctified thee, and I ordained thee a prophet unto the nations" (Jeremiah 1:5). John the Baptist was called by God to preach before he was born, and he leapt in his mother's womb as his mother, Elizabeth, was filled with the Holy Spirit (Luke 1:41).

The apostle Paul also had a keen sense of awareness about his destiny. He knew that God had plans for him even before his own birth! That's why Paul described the Father as the "...God, who separated me from my mother's womb, and called me by his grace, to reveal his Son in me, that I might preach him among the heathen..." (Galatians 1:15,16).

Both Jeremiah and Paul had a driving motivation, a strong will, and a determined attitude to do something great by fulfilling the purpose for which they were born into this world. One day when *your* race on this earth is over, the same should be said of you.

> Both Jeremiah and Paul had a driving motivation, a strong will, and a determined attitude to do something great by fulfilling the purpose for which they were born into this world.

There is something about knowing God's plan and purpose for one's life that gives a person a more focused sense of direction and provides a "bull's-eye" to aim at with the decisions he or she must make. Without this sense of direction, people have a tendency to flounder and wander aimlessly through life. This is precisely why Proverbs 29:18 says, "Where there is no vision, the people perish...." The *New International Version* says it this way: "Where there is no revelation, the people *cast off restraint*...."

The phrase "cast off restraint" paints a picture of people with no goal, no sense of direction, no purpose, no driving motivation, and no bull's-eye to target with their lives. Consequently, because they don't have any real sense of destiny, they "cast off restraint," wandering from one thing to another as they live selfishly and aimlessly unto themselves. And when their time on this earth is over, they leave this life without ever having accomplished anything significant or contributed much to the world.

This is exactly why the apostle Paul said, "Know ye not that they which in a race run all, but one receiveth the prize? So run, that ye may obtain. And every man that striveth for the mastery is temperate in all things. Now they do it to obtain a corruptible crown; but we an incorruptible. I therefore so run, not as uncertainly; so fight I, not as one that beateth the air" (1 Corinthians 9:24-26).

I want you to especially notice that Paul said, "...So run, that ye may obtain." This makes one thing crystal clear: *God wants you to obtain and fulfill your part in His plan!* It makes another truth very clear as well: In order for you to achieve what God has planned for your life, it is going to require some effort on *your* part!

PAUL'S RESOLVE

When runners run in a race, they have one goal before them and one thought foremost in their minds — reaching the finish line! With this illustration in mind, Paul tells us to run with all our might, keeping our focus on the finish line — fulfilling the purpose for our lives that has been revealed to us.

You might ask, "But how long am I to keep on running, striving, and trying?"

Paul said to keep running and working until you "obtain." The word "obtain" is the Greek word *katalambano*, which is a compound of two words, *kata* and *lambano*. This word is very similar to the word *katecho* (*hold fast*) that we studied in Chapter One. As you recall, the word *kata* describes *something that is coming downward*, and the word *lambano* means *to take or to seize something*. When compounded together into one word, these two words become *katalambano* — a word that has a powerful meaning.

This word "obtain" paints the picture of someone who finds something he has longed for his entire life. Rather than lose it or pass up the opportunity to possess it, he pounces on it with all his might, latching hold of it and seizing it with joy.

This word also carries the idea of a runner who runs fiercely with all his energy, straining forward toward the finish line. At last he reaches the goal and crosses the finish line. Now the prize is his because he gave that race all he had to give and ran with all the strength he could muster. The runner prepared; he trained; he strove — and all his determined effort paid off. Had he approached this opportunity lackadaisically, the prize would have gone to another. But because he ran to *obtain*, he now holds the prize in his hand!

Paul used his own life as an example, telling us that he was running this type of fierce spiritual race in order to fulfill his own destiny. Knowing he was called to preach, he did the unthinkable — even the unnecessary from time to time. Paul was willing to perform the most difficult of tasks, take the greatest of risks, and live a lifestyle of sacrifice — all for the purpose of doing what God had called him to do.

Paul had his focus set on his destiny like a runner who never takes his eyes off the finish line. Rather than approach his spiritual race lazily and halfheartedly, Paul did everything within his power to preach the Gospel as God had called him to do.

- If that meant getting a job on the side in order to be able to preach, that's what Paul did (Acts 18:3).

- If it meant becoming as a Jew in order to be able to preach to the Jews, that's what he did (1 Corinthians 9:20).

- If it meant becoming as those without the Law to win those who were without the Law, that's what he did (1 Corinthians 9:21).

- Paul became all things to all men for one purpose: that he might win as many as possible to the Lord (1 Corinthians 9:22).

Paul suffered hardship, persecution, lack, cold, hunger, nakedness, homelessness, trouble from false brethren, and trouble from true brethren. He suffered in the city, in the wilderness, and even in the sea. He was often afflicted by persecution, beaten, and troubled by religious people. Yet Paul never lost sight of the fact that he was born to fulfill his destiny.

> Paul never lost sight of the fact that he was born to fulfill his destiny.

Regardless of what came his way, Paul kept one thing foremost in his mind and preeminent in his thinking: *I must obtain the prize of the high calling of God in Christ Jesus. I must fulfill the purpose for which I was born. I must finish the race God has set before me in this life.* As he told the Philippians, "Not as though I had already attained, either were already perfect: but I follow after, if that I may apprehend that for which also I am apprehended of Christ Jesus" (Philippians 3:12).

If you want to achieve God's will for your life, you must live your life every day as Paul did — with an attitude of holy boldness and Holy Ghost-imparted determination. This alone will take you through the obstacles and attacks of the enemy, ultimately bringing you to the place God desires for your life.

I want you to notice one more thing that Paul said. He said, "I therefore so run, not as uncertainly; so fight I, not as one that beateth the air" (1 Corinthians 9:26). This tells us that Paul wasn't aimless or lacking in direction. He didn't keep trying this or that and then move on to try something else in an effort to figure out what he should be doing. Rather, Paul had direction. In every situation and at every turn, he sought God to know His perfect will and plan. Then Paul strove to carry out that divine plan exactly as the Holy Spirit revealed it to him.

Throughout his ministry, Paul displayed grit and backbone. He possessed resolve, strength of will, determination, courage, persistence, tenacity, and an unrelenting mindset. Paul was a no-nonsense kind of man who had put his foot down and taken his stand, putting his whole heart into his calling. He wasn't waiting for something to happen accidently. There was no "maybe I will, maybe I won't." Paul knew what God wanted, and he pursued God's plan with all his heart until the day came at the end of his life when he was able to say unequivocally, "I have finished my course" (2 Timothy 4:7).

What a triumphant testimony! This should be our goal in life as well. At the end of our lives, we should be able to look back with no regrets, knowing that even if we didn't do everything exactly right, we did the single most important thing correctly: We stayed on course, kept our sense of focus, and fulfilled God's primary purpose for our lives.

Unfortunately, many believers today lack the resolve and direction Paul possessed. They are aimless. They have no sense of direction and therefore accomplish very little, if anything, with their lives. Perhaps they even know what God wants, but they lack the resolve to keep pursuing that dream until it is fulfilled. Therefore, they live in uncertainty, as those who beat the air but never win the fight, or as those who halfheartedly run a race and therefore never win.

If you look back on what you have accomplished in life, you'll see that those achievements only happened because you set your heart on the goal and pursued it vigorously until it came to pass.

There's no doubt that you have a divine purpose or that God has placed His call on your life. He even planned your life before the foundation of the world. God has wonderful, marvelous ideas about you and your days on this earth! The important question is this: *Do you want to discover those divine ideas and commit your life to fulfilling them?*

If your answer is truly *yes*, let today be the day that you set your heart on achieving that goal. Don't let yourself be half-hearted, mealy-mouthed, or easily discouraged. It's time for some *resolve*!

You must maintain the attitude, "No matter what kind of attack the enemy tries or how great the obstacles become, I'm in this for the long haul. I'm not going to live my entire life missing what God has planned for me! Regardless of the inconvenience I have to endure, the price I must pay, or the adjustments I'm required to make in my attitudes, lifestyle, or future plans — I'm going to run this race, *and I'm going to win it*!"

> You must maintain the attitude, "No matter what kind of attack the enemy tries or how great the obstacles become, I'm in this for the long haul. I'm not going to live my entire life missing what God has planned for me!"

DREAM THIEF NUMBER FIVE:
NEUTRALITY

As you stand on your word from God and resolve to do all you need to do to fulfill that divine assignment, you need to be aware of another extremely sinister and sneaky enemy that will try to steal your dream from your heart. This wicked foe doesn't come from the devil, nor does it necessarily come from your friends or your family. This wretched enemy begins in your flesh. It is dream thief number five: *neutrality*!

Neutrality is one of the worst enemies you will ever face in this life. It is a dream thief that can insidiously worm its way into your life and overtake you without your even being aware of its presence.

As a believer, it's true that you have the power to overcome the works of the evil one and can have faith to remove mountains. But if you stay neutral in your walk with God, you will become spiritually sluggish as you gradually lose your inner drive and momentum — and, ultimately, you will let go of the God-given dream in your heart altogether.

> If you stay neutral in your walk with God, you will become spiritually sluggish as you gradually lose your inner drive and momentum — and, ultimately, you will let go of that God-given dream in your heart altogether.

So what exactly *is* neutrality? Let me answer that by first telling you how I came to understand the danger of this spiritual pitfall. For many, many years, I avoided one particular verse of Scripture because it contained a word that was totally repugnant to me: the word "slothful." Whenever I came to scriptures that spoke of slothfulness, I tried to avoid them, almost to the point of ignoring the presence of those scriptures in the Bible altogether.

For instance, whenever I read Hebrews 6, I'd usually skip right over verse 12 because it said, "That ye be not slothful, but followers of them who through faith and patience inherit the promises." It was unfortunate for me that I skipped over this verse for so many years because it contains powerful revelation that I desperately needed to avoid neutrality in my own spiritual walk — revelation that would help me fulfill the dream God had planted in my heart.

If you desire to fulfill your divine destiny, you need to hear, understand, and embrace Hebrews 6:12, because it exposes and explains this dream thief called neutrality. Had I not avoided this verse for all those years, I would have had the ammunition I needed much sooner to deal with this foul foe in my own life.

You may be wondering why I avoided this verse so adamantly and why I loathed the word "slothful" so much. Let me explain.

Living and enjoying life has never been a problem for me. I believe that God wants us to live life abundantly, free of man-made religious thinking and bondage. Pursuing the dreams God gives me has never been a problem for me either. The way I see it, a huge vision or a great challenge simply means an even greater victory on the other side and even more ground gained for the Kingdom of God. In fact, carrying out a mandate from God is my favorite thing to do!

Those who know me best are well aware that I'm not afraid to tackle the impossible or accept a challenge. My attitude is this: Since life is full of challenges anyway, why not choose to accept the challenges *God* sets before us and pursue them with all our might?

So with all that in mind, why have I had such an aversion to the concept of slothfulness or laziness? It goes back to a particular baseball coach I had when I was a very young boy.

This man had a son of his own who was on our team and who did quite well in baseball. I wasn't as gifted as his son, and the coach didn't particularly like me anyway, so I became a target on the baseball field.

The coach would continually press me to do more and more, and he often poked fun and embarrassed me in front of all the other players. He'd send me out onto the baseball field to play, but if I didn't perform just right (which I inevitably did not), he would say to me, "Rick, you're just lazy! You'll never be a good baseball player!" Again and again my coach would tell me, "You're just lazy! You're just lazy! You're just lazy!"

To further "encourage" me, the coach would often give me the thankless job of chasing everyone's foul balls. Needless to say, I was embarrassed and wanted to drop the sport altogether. I failed miserably at the sport of baseball, and, to this very day, I don't enjoy it very much.

However, the worst damage I suffered from that experience was caused by my coach's harassing statement, "You're just lazy!" I came to absolutely loathe and despise the word "lazy" — and whenever I read the word "slothful" in the Bible, I equated it with laziness. Every time I read Hebrews 6:12, I'd hear that baseball coach saying, "You're just *lazy*!"

Lazy is one thing I am not! After hearing all those accusations as a child from that baseball coach, I resolved that no one would ever be able to accuse me of laziness again. In fact, at times I went beyond the limits of my own bodily endurance just to stress the fact that I wasn't afraid of hard work or of taking on a challenge that looked too big. I would *not* have anyone accuse me of laziness! I even went to ridiculous lengths from time to time to prove my point and avoid being given that horrible label of "lazy."

But many years ago, I had an experience with the Lord that radically changed how I viewed this subject. While I was praying one day, the Lord spoke to my heart and said, "Rick, My plan for your life is being jeopardized by slothfulness."

"*What!*" I exclaimed. "Lord, You know I've been working hard! You know I've been writing books, teaching in seminars, and preaching in more than 300 meetings a year. How could You ever accuse me of laziness?"

The Holy Spirit gently answered me: "I didn't tell you that your ministry was being jeopardized by *laziness*. I said it was being jeopardized by *slothfulness*."

I was more shocked by the Holy Spirit's statement than if someone had walked up to me and slapped my face! I had worked so *hard* to get our ministry established, and Denise and I were finally beginning to see a measure of success. In fact, I'd been preaching and teaching in so many meetings that I'd begun to feel like a teaching, preaching machine. I almost felt that if someone pressed a button on me, a sermon would pop out of my mouth — without any thought on my part about what I was saying or doing! Yet despite all my hard work, the Lord had just told me that I was slothful!

Still in a state of shock, I decided to find out what the Holy Spirit meant by that statement. I turned to Hebrews 6:12 and, for the first time in my life, began to seriously study what the Bible means when it talks about "slothfulness." To my utter amazement, I discovered that, according to the Greek text, the word "slothful" didn't have anything to do with *laziness* at all. These two words aren't even minutely related or similar to each other. So I'd been avoiding this verse all those years for no reason!

The word "slothful" is taken from the Greek word *nothros* and describes something that is *slow* or *sluggish*. This word isn't talking about laziness; rather, it carries the idea of *something that has lost its speed or momentum*. It is still moving, but not with the same velocity and aggression it once possessed.

This word *nothros* could be typified by a candle that once burned brightly but whose dim flame doesn't shine like it once did. It could also describe a person who once felt very deeply about a certain goal and was wholeheartedly committed to achieving it — but whose passion is no longer what it was. Previously this person put all his time, effort, and attention into that cause, but now he doesn't even seem to care about it. His commitment to the dream has become slack, and his passion has begun to wear off. All of these descriptions provide an accurate portrayal of the Greek word *nothros*.

Thus, rather than painting a picture of laziness, *nothros* carries the idea of *neutrality*. It is a picture of:

- Something that is neither hot nor cold.

- Someone who is neither committed or uncommitted.

- An attitude or mentality that really couldn't care less anymore.

A person in this condition has lost his zeal, passion, and conviction for the vision or goal that once meant so much to him. Now he has become neutral. He doesn't care one way or the other, and he isn't moved by his convictions the way he once was. Although he is still inclined toward that dream, he no longer pursues its fulfillment the way he once did.

When I saw this meaning of the word *nothros* in the Greek text and finally understood the correct New Testament meaning of the word "slothful," I realized it would have been better if the Lord had told me that I was *lazy*! Slothfulness is far worse than laziness! Laziness is a mental and physical problem that can sometimes even be corrected by a change in diet and exercise habits. However, slothfulness goes far deeper than that. It is a spiritual problem that can only be corrected by the power of God following repentance.

I had been working and working and *working*, even to the point of overextending myself — and now the Lord was telling me that I'd become neutral right in the midst of all my hard efforts! As usual, after honestly examining my heart, I could see that the Lord was right.

When Denise and I first launched our traveling ministry, I had spent a great deal of time studying, praying, and fasting. But by the time the Lord talked to me during that prayer time, I had become a virtual ministry machine! If someone put me behind a pulpit, a message popped right out of me. If people lined up for prayer, I automatically prayed for them without giving it a second thought. Ministry no longer required any extra prayer or study time. It was just like working a regular job with a regular routine.

Although I had once vigorously studied the Word and diligently sought God for His anointing, I had since been reduced to a life with little personal spiritual growth or substance behind my public ministry. If I had continued in that state, it would have been only a matter of time before I lost tremendous ground in my spiritual life and floundered in my ability to minister. Outwardly I was busier than ever — but inwardly I had come to an intolerable state of stagnation.

Through this experience, I learned that neutrality has nothing to do with the amount of activity or the degree of faithfulness a person achieves externally. Slothfulness speaks of an *inward* neutral condition. When we're in neutral, it may outwardly look like we're going somewhere, but inwardly we are merely running in place like hamsters in a hamster wheel.

> Slothfulness speaks of an *inward* neutral condition. When we're in neutral, it may outwardly look like we're going somewhere, but inwardly we are merely running in place like hamsters in a hamster wheel.

DON'T LET YOUR FIRE GO OUT!

It is ironic that neutrality can set in more easily once we become extremely well-taught in God's Word. The more light we receive, the greater the potential for us to become neutral. Why is that?

Because too often we begin to think we know it all, and we replace our faith with knowledge.

Neutrality was the root problem in the Laodicean church (*see* Revelation 3:14-19). I call the Laodicean believers "the lopsided church" because they were "brain-heavy." They had all kinds of knowledge, but their fire had gone out. This is something God simply cannot fathom because He isn't neutral about *anything*. The Bible makes it all too clear that neutrality is something totally disgusting and repugnant to the Lord.

In Revelation 3:15 and 16, Jesus tells the pastor of the Laodicean church, "I know thy works, that thou art neither cold nor hot: I would thou wert cold or hot. So then because thou art lukewarm, and neither cold nor hot, I will spue thee out of my mouth."

First, Jesus says, "I know thy works." The Greek word for "know" is *oida*, which means *having intimate knowledge of someone*. Jesus is saying, "I know everything about you. I see everything you do. I know the motives and intents of your heart — every thought you think and every feeling you feel."

Jesus goes on to say, "...Thou art neither cold nor hot: I would thou wert cold or hot. So then because thou art lukewarm, and neither cold nor hot, I will spue thee out of my mouth." To understand what Jesus is saying here, we have to study the historical setting where the Laodicean believers lived.

The city of Laodicea was built in a region that was full of seismic activity and had experienced many earthquakes. As often happens in a seismic area, vents came up from the depths of the earth, allowing boiling hot water to reach the surface. In the nearby city of Hierapolis, these hot springs were famous. People came from great distances to bathe in those waters, believing they had medicinal powers. An experience in those waters was viewed to be therapeutic and effective in improving one's health.

Another city named Colossae was not too far away. As Hierapolis was known for its hot springs, Colossae was known for its cold waters. Just as people journeyed to Hierapolis to bathe in the hot springs for health purposes, people would travel great distances in the summer to vacation in Colossae, where they could invigorate themselves by taking frequent dips in the famous, refreshing, cool-to-freezing waters of that city.

Laodicea may have been the biggest and richest city in the area, but it had neither hot nor cold water. Therefore, the people of Laodicea had to leave their luxurious homes and travel to Colossae if they wanted to enjoy fresh, cool water. On the other hand, those who desired to soak in the hot springs had to travel six miles to Hierapolis.

Once in an attempt to bring the hot water from Hierapolis to Laodicea, the Romans commenced a huge construction project. The goal of those who initiated the project was to build pipes that would channel the hot water six miles from Hierapolis to the city of Laodicea. The pipes effectively delivered the water — a real feat of construction at that time. Sadly, however, the water lost its heat along the way. By the time the water reached Laodicea, it was not only lukewarm, but it had developed a sickening, nauseating taste. The taste was so revolting that no one wanted to drink it!

So when Jesus told the Laodiceans, "…Because thou art lukewarm, and neither cold nor hot, I will spue thee out of my mouth," this was a message that carried a strong punch. He was telling them, *"Because you have become so dead, dull, sickening and nauseating — because no spiritually refreshing waters flow from you, nor do you have any healing properties left — I will spew you out of My mouth!"*

The word "spew" is the Greek word *emeo*, and it means *to vomit, to spit out*, or *to regurgitate*. This picture of Jesus threatening to "spew" the Laodiceans out of His mouth doesn't mean He was *rejecting* or *disinheriting* them. It just reveals how utterly distasteful a spiritually lukewarm condition is to the Lord.

Have you ever eaten a spoonful of lukewarm soup or sipped a lukewarm drink that you expected to be piping hot? Even worse, have you ever taken an unexpected bite of a stale sandwich or a spoiled piece of fruit? The distastefulness of such an experience is a reflection of the repulsion God feels concerning the spiritual walk of a lukewarm Christian. With Him, there is no middle ground. He totally condemns a spiritual condition that allows one to remain neutral, noncommittal, and passive.

Because these Laodicean believers were lukewarm, they weren't good for anything in the work of God's Kingdom. They were not cool and refreshing, nor were they hot and healing. They were just stuck in the middle, like something that had lost both its flavor and its heat along the way.

Thus, verse 16 could be translated, *"Because you've lost your temperature and become lukewarm — because no refreshing waters flow out of you and you have no healing properties left — I find your taste in My mouth to be disgusting! I can't bear it anymore, and I have no choice but to spit you out!"*

When my ministry was first getting started, every fiber of my being ached to see the Spirit of God move when I preached or prayed for people. If someone got saved, healed, or filled with the Holy Spirit, I'd jump up and down, shout, and rejoice with them. But that fiery passion had dwindled by the time the Lord told me that I had become "slothful." I had seen so many miracles and supernatural works of God that I had allowed myself to lose my deep appreciation for those demonstrations of His power in people's lives.

I had become neutral, slothful, and lukewarm. You might say that I had begun to simply "traffic" in the things of God and had temporarily lost my sensitivity to discern what God was endeavoring to do through me. It had simply become "business as usual."

This is an abominable state for any believer to be in, but it is *especially* detestable for a minister of the Gospel!

Some people are absolutely passionate for God when they first experience the liberty of praise and worship and the power of the preaching and teaching of God's uncompromised Word. They can't wait to come to church every service; they can't get enough of the presence of the Holy Spirit during praise and worship; and they eagerly anticipate every one of the pastor's messages.

But as these same believers attend service after service, they gradually become accustomed to the freedom in praise and worship. As time passes, the music loses its excitement, and they rarely raise their hands to the Lord or get out of their seats to dance before Him. They still love God and desire to serve Him. However, they've become so acclimated to the new environment that they become numb to what the Holy Spirit is doing all around them. Sadly, this isn't an uncommon occurrence among Christians; it happens all the time.

Those of us who are ministers must especially be on our guard to keep ourselves from falling into a state of neutral slothfulness. Moving in the power of the Holy Spirit is our profession. We make our living with the things of God.

- We pray and hear from God.

- We prepare messages that cause others to grow in their spiritual walk.

- We move in the gifts of the Spirit.

- We pray for people and see God perform great and powerful miracles in their lives.

But if we're not careful, we can become neutral in our attitude toward these demonstrations of God's goodness and mercy. We can even begin to take His power for granted.

Again, it's ironic that where there is an abundance of blessing, the possibility of gradually sinking into a state of

> If we're not careful, we can become neutral in our attitude toward these demonstrations of God's goodness and mercy. We can even begin to take His power for granted.

slothfulness becomes greater. Like the self-sufficient Laodiceans, a church that has tremendous praise and worship, great preaching and teaching of God's Word, and a depth of understanding regarding the moving of the Holy Spirit is in more danger of becoming complacent than a church that is struggling to grow in these areas.

Why is this true? Because it's human nature to start taking for granted what comes easily to us. When we have to strive and work hard for something, we tend to appreciate it more. However, this is *human* nature, not *God's* nature.

God has the fullest appreciation at all times for the smallest, as well as the greatest, of His works. That's why He commands us not to be slothful in Hebrews 6:12. The Holy Spirit uses the imperative tense here, which means He is speaking in the strongest, most authoritative voice available in the Greek language. It is also a negative with a prohibition, which means that God is telling us, "Stop it — and *stop it right now!*"

The very fact that God commands us to stop being slothful tells us that there is something we can do to reverse this abominable condition. If we have become lukewarm or stagnant concerning the dream He has given us, *we* can do something about it. God has tossed the ball into our court, and now it's up to us.

SOMETHING ANYONE CAN DO

So how do we get out of this detestable state called neutrality? Or better still, how do we avoid it altogether?

Let's go back to Hebrews 6:12, where it says, "That ye be not slothful, but *followers* of them who through faith and patience inherit the promises." I want you to notice the word "followers." That word is taken from the Greek word *mimetes*, from which we get the English word "imitate." Other derivatives of this word are *mimeograph, mime, pantomime,* and *mimic.* But the word that best describes the meaning of *mimetes* in this verse is *actor.*

An actor is someone who skillfully and convincingly acts like someone else. So you could actually translate this phrase, "*...but skillfully and convincingly act like those who through faith and patience inherit the promises.*"

Since this is the true meaning of the word translated "followers" in Hebrews 6:12, we must ask the question, "What does an actor do?" An actor or actress studies the character and the lives of others and then portrays them on a stage or on film. If the actors are trying to portray real people, they will study written material about those individuals' lives: where they lived, how they talked, what kind of accent they had, what they accomplished with their lives, what their temperament was like, and so on.

A good actor will obtain every little bit of information he can about his subject in order to better portray him on the stage or screen. He will read everything he can about the person — and if that person is still alive, the actor may attempt an interview with his subject to get to know him even better. Then after the actor has gathered and assimilated all that information, he will begin to practice acting just like that person. He'll try to talk like him, think like him, walk like him, and dress like him. Throughout the course of the actor's day, he will ask himself, *What would this person do or say if HE were in this situation?*

After a while, a good actor will actually begin to resemble the individual he is imitating. As he moves into character, the actor learns to think, speak, and behave as though he really were his subject. It is as if he temporarily becomes that other person!

Years ago I was watching television and came across an interview with an actress who had recently played a demanding movie role — the part of a temperamental woman on the verge of insanity. The actress said that the role was extremely difficult and required her to continually practice the part. It was so emotionally taxing that she couldn't easily slip into character and then back out of character at the end of the day. Eventually she decided she'd stay in character all the time and behave as though she really were a temperamental, crazy woman.

At the end of three months, the filming was finished and the director said, "You can all go home now." But this actress had played her role without a break for so long that she went through a terrible identity crisis. The cameras were turned off and everyone else on the set had returned to their normal lives. But this woman was experiencing great difficulty in resuming her own identity. The role had actually become a part of her.

Such is the power of acting or imitating someone else! If you act long enough and consistently enough like that person, he or she will become a part of who you are.

Furthermore, *anyone* can act! Had the Bible said, "Fast from food for eight weeks, and then you can be delivered from neutrality," we may have rightly responded, "I can't fast for eight weeks." If the Bible had said, "Memorize 200 verses of Scripture, and then you can be delivered from neutrality," we may have had reason to say, "I don't have the ability to remember 200 verses of Scripture." But the writer of Hebrews didn't tell us to fast or memorize Scripture. He told us to "act" in order to reverse neutrality in our lives!

You may say, "But, Rick, I really don't know how to act! I'm just not an actor or an actress!" But the truth is, you *do* know how to act — everyone does!

- Children know exactly how to act when they want a new toy from their parents.

- Teenagers know exactly how to act when they want to avoid punishment.

- A wife knows how to act — how to look sweetly at her husband and speak in soft tones — when she wants to make her point.

- A husband knows how to act when he wants to do something his wife may not be in total agreement with.

Many years ago, I was driving down the road with one of my sons, who was four years old at the time. He began to wistfully say, "Oh, Daddy, I want to preach like you preach. I want to travel with you. I want to lead people to Jesus."

When I heard those words, my heart began to melt. For a moment, I was overcome with emotion. My young son had said the words I most wanted to hear from him. He was expressing my greatest desire and dream for his life!

But before I could formulate and utter a reply, my dear, beloved son added hopefully, "Daddy, can I have a new toy today?"

Oh, yes, my four-year-old son definitely knew how to act!

Everyone, from the very young to the very old, knows how to act. It is innate, a part of human nature.

Understanding the power of imitation, the writer of Hebrews essentially said, "If you've become neutral, find people who are still on fire and watch what they say, how they behave, and how they live — and then act like them! Do what they do, say what they say, and behave like they behave. Be imitators of them who through faith and patience have inherited the promises!"

Someone may ask, "But isn't it hypocritical to do that? Isn't it wrong to act like you feel great when you really feel terrible?" Absolutely not! Acting and imitating is foundational to the Christian life. It is for this very reason we are told, "...Put ye on the Lord Jesus Christ, and make not provision for the flesh..." (Romans 13:14).

Do you know why we're commanded to put on the Lord Jesus Christ? Because if we *don't* decide to put on the character of Christ, we will make provision for the flesh. Putting on Christ is a daily decision, and it leads to a daily mindset.

So wake up each morning and declare that you have the mind of Christ. Determine to act like who you truly are in the Spirit — a new creation with the nature, character, desires, and behavior of Jesus Christ. Act like Jesus!

> Wake up each morning and declare that you have the mind of Christ. Determine to act like who you truly are in the Spirit — a new creation with the nature, character, desires, and behavior of Jesus Christ.

MORE THAN AN IMPERSONATION

It would be wrong, however, to simply leave you with the impression that you are to live your life impersonating other people. Hebrews 6:12 tells you to be a *follower* of those who through faith and patience inherit the promises. But in order to fully understand the meaning of this verse, you must understand Hebrews 13:7 as well. It says, "Remember them which have the rule over you, who have spoken unto you the word of God: whose faith follow, considering the end of their conversation." I want you to particularly notice the last half of the verse: "...whose faith follow, considering the end of their conversation."

God commands us to be "followers," "actors," and "imitators" of those whom He has placed in authority over us. That does *not* mean He is encouraging personality cults! It isn't the *personalities* of other people we are to follow or imitate — it is *their faith*!

How do you know if certain people possess the kind of faith worth imitating? The writer of Hebrews tells us in the last part of this verse: "...considering the end of their conversation." In other words, he is saying, "Look at their lives!"

- When all is said and done, what have their lives produced?

- Do they consistently demonstrate the fruit of the Spirit?

- Have they won battles and gained territory for the Kingdom of God, in spite of the difficult times they've faced?

If the answer to these questions is *yes*, their faith is worthy of serious consideration.

People who produce godly results despite hardship and difficult times are well worth our attention and contemplation. These are the people we are commanded to seek out and imitate. But remember — *we're not imitating their personalities; we're imitating their faith*. We've seen that their faith is the kind that endures, produces a harvest, and has a good end!

In Chapter Two, I wrote of Christians who simply repeat what others say like parrots. The mistake some people make is to just mindlessly say and do what someone else says and does. But that emphatically is *not* what I'm talking about here, and this common mistake doesn't dismiss the importance of truly following the faith of someone else. I'm speaking of developing a genuine faith as you see it demonstrated in someone else's life.

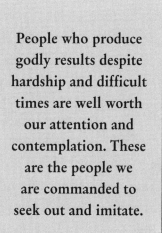

People who produce godly results despite hardship and difficult times are well worth our attention and contemplation. These are the people we are commanded to seek out and imitate.

Locate people who have tackled the odds, come against opposition, and perhaps even made blunders of their own. Yet despite all they've gone through, they still believe God and they're still pursuing the dream He placed in their hearts. Don't focus so much on the actions of these individuals; *instead, endeavor to imitate their attitude of determined, steadfast faith in the face of every obstacle.*

When you encounter people who fit this description, get to know them. Find out how they manage to spend time with God and their families and still remain committed and involved in the local church. Find out how they have developed their faith. Watch them worship; watch them give; watch how they respond to different situations. And if you determine that their lives are faith-filled and worthy of imitating, begin to act like these individuals as you face your own challenges in life. Remember their example as you follow the apostle Paul's admonition to the Philippian church: "Those things, which ye have both learned, and received, and heard, and seen in me, do: and the God of peace shall be with you" (Philippians 4:9).

Now, let me just warn you: As you begin to live a life of faith, acting on what you believe and not on what you see or feel, the devil will immediately and repeatedly accuse you of being a two-faced hypocrite. He will bombard your mind with negative thoughts, telling you that you're a complete fake and that you don't really think or feel the way you're talking and acting.

But you can answer the devil truthfully and still remain in faith. Just say, "That's right, Satan, my thoughts and emotions don't always line up with what I'm saying and doing by faith. However, I'm imitating those who don't live their lives by what they see or feel but by what God has said in His Word. I'm following those who have fire and zeal in their hearts so I can develop the same fire and zeal in my own life!"

This is a vital aspect of discipleship. We are to act like those whose lives are worthy examples of godliness and faith — to follow those individuals as they follow Christ.

Paul said of Timothy, in effect, "If you've seen Timothy, you've seen me! He thinks like me, he acts like me, and he will care for you as I care for you" (*see* Philippians 2:20). Why did Paul say that? Because Timothy had grown up spiritually with Paul. He had been discipled by Paul, walking with him and ministering with him through all kinds of situations.

Thus, Timothy was a real-life example of what happens when a person imitates the faith of a seasoned, faith-filled person. Timothy knew exactly what Paul was talking about when the apostle said to his followers on numerous occasions, "You know my life; you have seen me in all situations" (*see* Acts 20:18-21) and

"Be ye followers of me, even as I also am of Christ" (1 Corinthians 11:1).

ACTING LIKE JESUS

What about you? What would just one day of your life be like if you committed yourself to think, speak, and act just like Jesus in every situation you faced that day?

In Ephesians 5:1, Paul exhorts, "Be ye therefore followers [*mimetes*] of God, as dear children." An appropriate way to paraphrase that verse would be, *"Act like God. Imitate Him like little children imitate their father."*

So what is God like?

- His power, gifts, and abilities are limitless.

- He knows exactly who He is and what His plans and purposes are.

- His knowledge and wisdom are at the heart of every decision He makes, and His Word is His absolute bond.

- When He makes a promise, He will stand by it 100 percent.

- If His promise is conditional, He will make it perfectly and abundantly clear what needs to be done in order for that promise to be fulfilled.

- His prized possession and the apple of His eye are the believers who give their lives into His care; yet He will do everything within His power to save, heal, and deliver those who rebel against Him.

- He loves people unconditionally because He chooses to do so.

- He is bold and powerful, yet kind and selfless.

This brief description of God only begins to scratch the surface of who and what He is. But with these qualities in mind, take some time to ask yourself: *What would happen to my life, my family, my church, my community, my nation, and the world if I received a revelation of what it really means to "act like God"? Would my fire and zeal for the things of God be restored — or could I keep it from ever being lost in the first place?*

> Ask yourself: *What would happen to my life, my family, my church, my community, my nation, and the world if I received a revelation of what it really means to "act like God"?*

Again, everyone has the capacity to act, no matter what his or her circumstances or situation. That's just how God is. He meets His people on a level they can understand and gives them a strategy that is easily put into practice. Not everyone can evangelize on the streets or go on the mission field to feed and clothe the needy, but anyone can act!

If you'd just decide to smile all day and act as though you were totally fulfilled and content with life, you'd be amazed at how that one decision can affect your attitude and your life in general. In fact, scientists have proven that the configuration of your mouth can affect the attitude of your mind. Tests have shown that people who frown are always sad and those who smile have a more positive outlook on life.

How is it possible to go through each day acting like your life is filled with God's blessing and favor, even in the midst of difficult times? By following Paul's exhortation to the Philippian church:

> **Finally, brethren, whatsoever things are true, whatsoever things are honest, whatsoever things are just, whatsoever things are pure, whatsoever things are lovely, whatsoever things are of good report; if there be any virtue, and if there be any praise, think on these things. Those things, which ye have both learned, and received, and heard, and seen in me, do: and the God of peace shall be with you.**
>
> **Philippians 4:8,9**

So look for those you can follow — those who have learned to walk by faith, no matter what challenge they faced. In the midst of fiery trials, these people chose to set their minds on what God already said and then to speak and act according to His words, not according to what they saw or felt. You must do the same.

Is Anyone Worthy of Imitation?

At this point, many believers throw up their hands in frustration and sigh, "But I don't know anyone who is worthy of imitation." My answer to that is again found in Hebrews 13:7, which says, "Remember them which have the rule over you, who have spoken unto you the word of God: whose faith follow, considering the end of their conversation [the results and fruit of their way of life]."

This verse of Scripture commands you to follow those whom God has placed in leadership over you ("which have rule over you") and who feed you the Word of God ("who have spoken unto you the word of God"). This would primarily refer to your pastor and associate pastors. However, it would also include others in the local church who are in leadership, such as Sunday schoolteachers, the choir director, the head usher, the director of counseling, etc. Finally, it would include other ministers to whom God has connected you and from whom you regularly receive the ministry of the Word.

However, here's something extremely important for you to remember: These leaders are real people with real problems of their own — and when you discover they're not perfect, the enemy will tempt you to back away from your involvement in the church. But if God has called you to that local body of believers and directed you to a particular area of service in the church, the Bible tells you to stay put and *imitate the Christ-likeness* in those leaders, no matter how imperfect they are.

Years ago after one of my meetings, a couple walked over to me and said, "Brother Rick, we need a word from the Lord." They flipped on their tape recorder, stuck it in my face, and waited expectantly for an anointed, powerful prophecy to flow from my lips.

I asked them, "Where do you go to church?"

They answered, "Well, we don't go to church. We've been looking for a church but just haven't been able to find one in this town."

I asked, "Oh, are you new here?"

"Well," they replied, "we're not originally from here."

"Oh, how long have you lived here, then?"

"Sixteen years."

Sixteen years! I thought in disbelief. Immediately I said, "I have a word from God for you!"

The tape recorder clicked on as they thrust it up to my face again. I said, "The Lord says: 'Repent of your arrogance, rebellion, and pride, and get rooted and grounded in a local church!'"

"Is that all?" they asked.

"I doubt that you will get another word from God until you obey this one," I told them sternly.

So many Christians move from church to church, trying to find perfect leadership. They see someone else's humanity and then run for the hills. That's why when people come to work for this ministry, the first thing Denise and I do is tell them how human we are. We relate to them some of the mistakes we've made and admit that we'll probably make many more in the future. We tell them that we're flawed human beings with faults, weaknesses, and problems to work out just like everyone else.

The reason we do this with all our employees is to burst any bubbles and dispel any misguided notion they might have that all ministers are almost perfect. Too often people assume that, because ministers are powerfully anointed to preach or to fill their position of leadership, that means they live their lives "without spot or wrinkle." Certainly that should be our goal, but we're not there yet, and we don't know anyone else who is either!

Christian leaders are just imperfect human beings who have been placed into a position of responsibility because God found them faithful. *And it is precisely because God has found those leaders faithful that you should find them worthy of imitation.*

The people God has placed in leadership over you are not perfect in everything they say and do. They don't always control their temper. They sometimes miss the mark. How do I know this? Because there have never been any perfect people except Jesus Himself!

However, the men and women whom God considers worthy of your imitation are people who willingly enter the fight of faith on a daily basis, practicing the Word of God and following the leading of the Holy Spirit to the best of their strength, ability, and understanding. They stay in the battle and continue to fight, regardless of whether they win or lose a skirmish along the way. There is something noble and godly about their tenacity to keep on long after others have given up. These are the saints of God worth imitating. Following their faith will help you sustain the fire in your heart as you set your sights on the finish line of your own God-ordained course!

Think About It

Just as a rudder steers the course of a ship, your divine purpose provides a sense of direction to steer the course of your life. Are your habits and immediate goals consistent with your life's purpose? If not, those habits and goals, although well-meaning, can pull you off course.

Are you investing the necessary time and cultivating the kind of good habits that will draw you closer to your dream — or are you allowing bad habits to remain that pull you further away from its fulfillment?

The busyness of daily life can sometimes serve as a distraction that hinders us from becoming the kind of people we ultimately want to be. It is possible to "multi-task" ourselves into a state of unproductiveness as a result of nearly nonstop activity.

What activities in your life are colliding to prevent you from following God's plan for your life to the fullest?

Patience and passivity are two different positions of heart, although their external act of waiting may look the same. Patience is a controlled and decisive stillness that waits with confident expectation for a desired end. Passivity, on the other hand, simply waits and shifts position based on the influence of external forces rather than internal decisions. Passivity will extinguish the embers of your passion.

If you've been waiting on your dream, have you been waiting with patience and passionate expectation? Or have you lost the fire of purpose, allowing yourself instead to just passively float along in neutral — lukewarm and disconnected from your dream?

CHAPTER FIVE

A BIBLICAL PATRIARCH WORTH IMITATING

*A*fter reading the last chapter, you may be thinking, *I seriously can't think of anyone I personally know who is worth imitating — who possesses noble qualities and an outstanding character and who just keeps on going, no matter what the odds or how many mistakes he or she makes.*

If you can't think of anyone in your life who fits that description, let me give you a biblical character to imitate — a man named Abraham. This was a man whom the Word of God specifically designated as worthy of imitation.

> **For when God made promise to Abraham, because he could swear by no greater, he sware by himself, Saying, Surely blessing I will bless thee, and multiplying I will multiply thee. And so, after he had patiently endured, he obtained the promise.**
>
> **Hebrews 6:13-15**

In verse 12, the Holy Spirit directs us to be "...followers [imitators] of them who through faith and patience inherit the promises." Then in the very next verses, He gives Abraham as an example for us to follow.

But why is Abraham someone we should imitate? Frankly, if he were alive today and had made the mistakes he committed during his lifetime, I seriously doubt that a pastor would ask Abraham to be a guest speaker in his church or that Christians would go hear him in a seminar. On the other hand, given the dramatic nature of some of those mistakes, we might hear a lot about Abraham on the evening news!

Think about it. In order to save his own skin, Abraham put his wife in a bad position on two different occasions — one in which she might have been required to sleep with another man. In doing so, Abraham opened the door for his son, Isaac, to make the very same mistake years later (*see* Genesis 26:7)!

With all this in mind, I ask the question again: *Why did the Bible give us Abraham as a believer to imitate?*

GOD'S CALL TO ABRAM:
THREE SIMPLE COMMANDS AND FOUR PROMISES

When Abraham was first called of God, he was called Abram, and we know from the account in Genesis that he originally lived in an area called Ur of the Chaldees. In Acts 7, Stephen spoke to the Sanhedrin of a dramatic visitation from God that Abram experienced in Ur that would forever change him — separating him and calling him into a new life.

> **And he [Stephen] said, Men, brethren, and fathers, hearken; The God of glory appeared unto our father Abraham, when he was in Mesopotamia, before he dwelt in Charran [Haran], and said unto him, Get thee out of thy country, and from thy kindred, and come into the land which I shall shew thee. Then came he out of the land of the Chaldaeans, and dwelt in Charran: and from thence, when his father was dead, he removed him into this land, wherein ye now dwell.**
>
> **Acts 7:2-4**

Acts 7:2 tells us that one day the God of glory appeared to Abram. The Greek word for "appear" *is phaneroo*, which refers to *something that was invisible but has now come into plain view and appears exactly as it truly is.* In other words, this was no fake cloud of smoke that Abram saw. This was the Shekinah glory — the cloud of the presence of Almighty God in all His splendor and power!

We know from Galatians 3:8 (*NKJV*) that on this particular day in the land of Ur, the mighty voice of God came resounding out of that glory cloud as He preached the Gospel to Abram.

> **And the Scripture, foreseeing that God would justify the Gentiles by faith, preached the gospel to Abraham beforehand, saying, "In you all the nations shall be blessed."**

Then God proceeded to give Abram certain directives and promises, all of which we find in Genesis 12:1-3.

Now the Lord had said unto Abram, Get thee out of thy country, and from thy kindred, and from thy father's house, unto a land that I will shew thee: And I will make of thee a great nation, and I will bless thee, and make thy name great; and thou shalt be a blessing: and I will bless them that bless thee, and curse him that curseth thee: and in thee shall all families of the earth be blessed.

God had given Abram three life-altering commands. Abram was to:

1. Leave his country — Ur of the Chaldees.

2. Leave his family, which meant taking only his wife, Sarai, with him.

3. Go to a new land that the Lord would give to Abram and his descendants.

God also made four promises to Abram, which were dependent on Abram's ability to obey His commands:

1. God would give Abram a child, through whom He would make of Abram a great nation.

2. God would make Abram's name great.

3. He would bless Abram.

4. Through Abram, all the families of the earth would be blessed.

These were simple, uncomplicated, easy-to-understand directives and promises. However, of the commands and promises God gave Abram, Abram responded correctly to only one of them: *He left his country.* Everything else he thoroughly messed up! What happened?

First, although Abram did leave Ur of the Chaldees (the one command he got absolutely right), he didn't leave behind all his relatives and take only his wife Sarai and his servants with him. Instead, he also brought his nephew Lot, as well as Lot's family and servants along on the journey.

It's possible that, after his brother Haran died in Ur, Abram had adopted his nephew Lot according to ancient custom. This may have been why Abram felt justified in taking Lot and his group with them. Perhaps Abram assumed that, since Sarah was barren, the seed to bless nations would come from the loins of his adopted nephew.

But Abram didn't stop there; he also brought along his father Terah, the patriarch of the family, and all of his father's entourage as well. *Certainly,* Abram probably reasoned, *God wouldn't want me to leave my honored father behind!* This was a significant matter that Abram had to grapple with because of the customs of the time. Leaving his father would have brought great shame upon him in the eyes of men and destroyed his reputation.

So besides their own servants, Abram and Sarai came out of Ur not only with their nephew Lot and all of Lot's family and servants, but also with Terah and all of *his* family members and servants! Some Bible scholars speculate that Abram's full entourage must have numbered several hundred people. God had said, "You must leave your kindred and countrymen behind, Abram" — yet Abram ultimately left with hundreds. It was a good thing Abram was rich, because it required a lot of money to take such a huge caravan on this journey!

What had happened that caused Abram to disobey the Lord's simple directive? Abram began to interpret the word of the Lord he had been given in the light of his own understanding. As a result, he convinced himself that it was acceptable to take his adopted nephew, Lot, and his revered father, Terah, with him and leave the rest of his family behind.

> What had happened that caused Abram to disobey the Lord's simple directive? Abram began to interpret the word of the Lord he had been given in the light of his own understanding.

But Abram's disobedience had just begun. After his company traveled a relatively short distance, they stopped at the city of Haran rather than traveling on to the land God had promised Abram. Some scholars speculate that the journey was interrupted because Abram's father became ill. Abraham and his entire entourage were then forced to wait in the city of Haran for five years while his father slowly died (Acts 7:4).

Abram was learning that, if we don't fully obey a word from God, we mess up His timing and leave ourselves vulnerable to the attacks of the enemy.

When Abram's father finally died, Abram gathered his huge entourage and left to continue his journey to Canaan.

Unfortunately, when they arrived in the Promised Land, this wonderful land of promise was in the midst of a terrible famine, and there was no way the land could support all the people and livestock that had accompanied Abram and Sarai.

If Abram and Sarai had traveled to Canaan by themselves as God had commanded, there would have been enough food to feed them. However, there was definitely *not* enough food and land to provide for the multitude of people, camels, goats, and other livestock that Abram had brought into the land.

To solve this dilemma, Abram decided they should go down to Egypt, where there was plenty of food. The only problem was that Pharaoh was quite a ladies' man and had been known to kill men for their wives. Therefore, in fear for his life, Abram convinced Sarai to say she was his sister — even to the point of becoming one of Pharaoh's wives and possibly sleeping with Pharaoh if necessary. (Think of it! This was the man later called the Father of Faith! Would you have him in *your* church?)

But Pharaoh soon became aware of this charade and promptly kicked Abram's entire company out of Egypt. Once back in the land of famine, Abram and Lot found that the parched earth couldn't support their vast herds of livestock, so Abram came up with another idea. Lot and his family, servants, and livestock would go one way (with Lot choosing the direction), and Abram and his family, servants, and livestock would go the other way.

Almost immediately after the two families parted, Lot got himself into trouble. He was taken captive by five foreign kings, and Abram had to start a war in order to save him (*see* Genesis chapter 14). To Abram's great dismay, he and his men had to wage a war that never would have occurred if he had not disobeyed God at the beginning of the journey by bringing Lot with him to the Promised Land.

SEEING IS BELIEVING

By the fifteenth chapter of Genesis, Abram's father had gotten sick and died; Abram's group had reached the land of promise, only to find a famine; they had been kicked out of Egypt; and they had been through a war. Abram probably felt like he couldn't take one more step. But right in the midst of feeling discouraged and ready to quit, Abram had another encounter with God.

> After these things the word of the Lord came unto Abram in a vision, saying, Fear not, Abram: I am thy shield, and thy exceeding great reward. And Abram said, Lord God, what wilt thou give me, seeing I go childless, and the steward of my house is this Eliezer of Damascus? And Abram said, Behold, to me thou hast given no seed: and, lo, one born in my house is mine heir.
>
> And, behold, the word of the Lord came unto him, saying, This shall not be thine heir; but he that shall come forth out of thine own bowels shall be thine heir. And he brought him forth abroad, and said, Look now toward heaven, and tell the stars, if thou be able to number them: and he said unto him, So shall thy seed

be. And he believed in the Lord; and he counted it to him for righteousness.

Genesis 15:1-6

When God declared His protection and provision for Abram in verse 1, Abram went "nose to nose" with God in his complete frustration. He asked God where the baby was that He had promised, since the only child who had been born in his tent was the son of Eliezer, his servant!

To strengthen and establish Abram's faith, God told him, "Look at the stars in the heavens, and try to count them. As many as you can see — so shall your seed be" (v. 5). In other words, God gave Abram a mental picture or image of what He had promised him. Suddenly Abram *saw* it. He understood what God was trying to say to him, and the Bible says it was at this exact moment that Abram believed God.

There is something about *seeing* — visualizing, dreaming, and imagining — what God has promised us that causes faith to rise up in our hearts and sustain us in difficult times. We should never underestimate the power of the images and dreams God places in our hearts and minds. Those mental pictures cause us to believe in His promises all the more fervently and to continue walking in faith, just as was true in Abram's life.

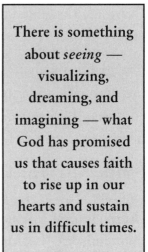

There is something about *seeing* — visualizing, dreaming, and imagining — what God has promised us that causes faith to rise up in our hearts and sustain us in difficult times.

COVENANT WITH THE CREATOR

After that moment when Abram chose to believe in God's promise and to commit his entire life to obeying Him, the Lord told him, "I'm going to cut a covenant with you." Then God said, "...Take me an heifer of three years old, and a she goat of three years old, and a ram of three years old, and a turtledove, and a young pigeon" (Genesis 15:9).

So Abram began to gather all the pieces of meat that were necessary to cut a covenant with Almighty God Himself. After killing the animals, Abram cut each carcass down the middle, breaking them in half and laying the pieces in the right order. Preparing to cut a blood covenant was a great ordeal!

After all the pieces of the sacrifice were laid out, the ritual required the two parties cutting covenant to walk between the pieces in a figure-eight configuration. This symbolic act declared that these two individuals had died unto themselves and become one — similar to the concept of the marriage covenant.

Abram finished preparing the animal sacrifice and then began to wait and *wait* for God to show up. Long hours passed, and verse 11 says that Abram spent the time chasing away the birds that came to eat the sacrifice.

Finally, God arrived on the scene, but not as Abram expected. Genesis 15:12 says, "And when the sun was going down, a deep sleep fell upon Abram; and, lo, an horror of great darkness fell upon him." A "horror of great darkness" was an Old Testament expression that described a paralyzing force. Although a person was able to see and hear, he wasn't able to move. Abram, the man who was always busy and industrious, was temporarily frozen in his tracks.

Then after God had gotten Abram's full attention and had totally immobilized him, He did a remarkable thing. The Lord actually took Abram's place in the cutting of the covenant!

Verse 17 says, "And it came to pass, that, when the sun went down, and it was dark, behold a smoking furnace, and a burning lamp that passed between those pieces." A "smoking furnace" and a "burning lamp" were Old Testament expressions that denoted the presence of God.

So after Abram did all that work to prepare the covenant sacrifice — after he waited and waited for God to show up, chasing away birds for hours — God finally appeared. But now Abram was frozen and couldn't move! He could see what God was doing; he could hear what He was saying. But no matter how hard Abram tried, he could not move to walk through the pieces with the Lord.

So God walked the figure-eight configuration alone among those dead, bloody carcasses — taking Abram's place and essentially cutting the covenant with Himself.

God had immobilized Abram so that Abram could not be a part of this covenant ritual. Then as soon as God had finished, He released Abram's body.

Many Christians believe that Abram cut the covenant with God. But if they were to look at this passage more closely, they'd discover that he did not! To cut covenant, a person had to walk through the dead pieces with the other covenant partner, and Abram didn't do this.

Why didn't God want Abram to be a part of this covenant? Because Abram had a track record of messing up everything He had asked him to do, and God knew that eventually Abram would break the covenant as well. So God temporarily paralyzed him and in effect told him, "Abram, I'm doing this one by Myself."

The Bible says in Hebrews 6:13, "For when God made promise to Abraham, because he could swear by no greater, he sware by himself." When God made covenant with Himself and swore by Himself, the covenant could not be broken "...because he could swear by no greater...." Now God was bound to use Abram in His plan of redemption, whether He wanted to or not, and to fulfill His promises to him.

Thousands of years later, Jesus did the same thing when He established a New Covenant. On the Cross Jesus took our place and offered Himself as the perfect Sacrifice for our sins. If we had crawled up on that Cross with Jesus, we would have had the power to break the covenant He was cutting with Himself to atone for our sins. In the past 2,000 years of Church history, Christians have given Jesus plenty of reasons to abandon the whole plan of redemption and just start over. But because Jesus cut a blood covenant on the Cross with Himself, He has to fulfill that covenant.

That's why the gifts and callings of God are without repentance. God was bound by Himself to supernaturally transform childless

Abram into *Abraham*, the father of many nations. In the same way, Jesus Christ is bound by Himself to use us — imperfect members of His Body with faults and weaknesses — to carry out His plans and purposes.

> God was bound by Himself to supernaturally transform childless Abram into *Abraham*, the father of many nations.

Wrong Again, Abram!

What do you suppose Abram's response to this profound experience? It's possible that he jumped up, ran down the hill, and told everyone, "I met God! And guess what? *I'm going to have a baby!*"

At this point, we can safely imagine that Sarai may have asked, "By the way, Abram, did God say anything about *me* while you were up there?"

Abram may have answered, "You know, Sweetheart, come to think of it, the Lord never even mentioned your name."

So once again, Abram and Sarai interpreted the word of the Lord in light of their own natural understanding. Sarai suggested that Abram sleep with her servant, Hagar (probably acquired during Abram's first rendezvous of disobedience in Egypt).

So Hagar conceived and bore Abram's child; however, the birth of this son caused nothing but strife in Abram's household, for now the servant girl could claim a position of honor in Abram's life — as the mother of his son — that Sarai could not.

The family problems continued to escalate after the child Ishmael was born, but God would not yet allow Abram to reject this son. In fact, Ishmael was 13 years old before God appeared to Abram and Sarai, changed their names to Abraham and Sarah, and declared that, within the year, *they* would have the promised child.

After Isaac was born to Abraham and Sarah, God then reinforced Sarah's demand to throw Hagar and Ishmael out of the camp. Yet even then, He promised His protection and provision to Ishmael and to his descendants — represented today by the Arab nations.

It's sobering to realize the enormous consequences that have resulted from Abraham's decision to bear a son through the slave girl, Hagar. All the conflicts in the Middle East over the years between Israel and her Arab neighbors can be traced back to that decision — to their common forefather's fleshly attempt to bring about the promise of God on his own.

THE FATHER OF FAITH?

Everybody talks about "the great faith of Abraham" and how Abraham believed God for several decades. But my question is this: Why did it take so long for the divine promise of a son to finally come to pass in Abraham's life? The answer is obvious: Because with every step he took, Abraham messed up the plan of God. *That's* why it took so long!

- God had said, "I want you and Sarai to come alone to a new land that I will show you." But instead, Abram brought his father and his nephew, Lot — a decision that delayed God's plan.

- God said, "You are going to have a son," so Abram slept with Hagar — another decision that delayed the plan of God for several more years.

By his own choices, Abraham personally delayed God's will for his life for many, many years. Why in the world, then, does the Bible use Abraham as an example of someone we should imitate? Because with every mistake he made, with every wrong turn he took, and with every gross error in judgment, Abraham never lost his passion or ceased to wholeheartedly continue to follow the Lord.

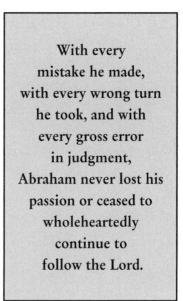

> With every mistake he made, with every wrong turn he took, and with every gross error in judgment, Abraham never lost his passion or ceased to wholeheartedly continue to follow the Lord.

According to his own limited level of knowledge and understanding, Abraham believed he was doing everything in his power to fulfill God's will for his life. He may have missed it by miles, but he was still following after the voice of God. In other words, it wasn't Abraham's behavior or actions we are to imitate; *it was his steadfast zeal for God.*

Don't look for a perfect person to imitate, because you're not going to find one other than the Lord Jesus Christ. Instead, look for believers who have an ever-burning flame in their hearts for God — who maintain their fire through the years and through all manner of adversity. Like Abraham, these people will be found in the "Hall of Faith."

Look for a believer who refuses to release the dream in his or her heart and who perseveres until that dream is fulfilled. *That* is a faith worthy of imitation!

THINK ABOUT IT

Abraham interpreted the word of the Lord in light of his own understanding and the expectations of others. As a result, he veered off course, failed to fully obey, and ultimately brought unnecessary difficulty upon both himself and his family.

Consider some specific directions the Lord has given you. Have you fully obeyed what you know to be His will for your life? Do you recognize some unpleasant consequences spilling over into the lives of others as a result of your own disobedience? If so, simply repent and ask the Father of mercies to direct your path according to His perfect will. Then step out and do whatever He tells you to do.

The provision and blessing God has for you is directly related to the course He has ordained for you to follow. Any detours from that course will also affect the timing in which God's plan will come to pass. Partial obedience (which is, in truth, simply disobedience) delays the will of God for your life and makes you vulnerable to the attacks of the enemy.

Take some time to get quiet before the Lord and be honest with yourself. Have you allowed doubt or fear to hinder you — to adversely affect your obedience and steer you off course?

God took Abraham's place to guarantee the effectiveness of the blood covenant He made on Abraham's behalf. Jesus took your place to become a surety and a guarantee of a better covenant.

God has gone to great lengths to ensure your success. What steps have you taken to provide a return on His matchless investment into your life?

CHAPTER SIX

FAITH AND PATIENCE: A MARRIAGE MADE IN HEAVEN

*T*here is nothing more exhilarating than receiving a word or a dream from the Lord. When we first wake up to the call of God on our lives, a kind of natural excitement — a sense of happiness and fulfillment — floods into our souls because we've finally discovered what God wants for us!

However, a dream often takes time to come to pass. And as the dream thieves begin to assault and malign our word from God, that natural, easily attained "happiness" can quickly dissipate and dissolve in the face of discouragement and opposition. When those warm, happy emotions begin to wane, we can find ourselves asking, *If my dream is really from God, why is it taking so long to manifest? Just how long am I supposed to wait for it to come to pass?*

I frequently hear from people who ask such questions. Although they are sure they heard from God, they need further encouragement, instruction, and insight on how to receive their promise.

These people often tell me, "I know that God spoke to me! It was the clearest word I've ever received in my life. My pastor and my spouse both agree I heard from God, but nothing has happened yet. Am I doing something wrong? I've tried really hard to do everything right. I've been careful to make positive confessions of faith. I've given my tithes and offerings. I've prayed and sought God. I've even stepped out in faith and begun to take measures to move toward my goal. But how long am I supposed to wait? Am I supposed to put my whole life on hold until this dream comes to pass? Please tell me, what am I doing wrong?"

Hearing from God and receiving His divine dream for your life is the easy part. It's quite another thing, however, to wait in faith and patience until you see that word from Heaven come to fruition. As you hold fast, you must wrestle with all the dream thieves — time, the devil, friends, family, and your own insecurities. And when these dream thieves work together, they can muster quite a fight against your soul!

> Hearing from God and receiving His divine dream for your life is the easy part. It's quite another thing, however, to wait in faith and patience until you see that word from Heaven come to fruition.

Discouragement can set in for a number of reasons as you pursue your vision. Perhaps you expected the fulfillment of your dream to happen quickly, but, instead, it has taken time. Or maybe you hoped others would rejoice about your vision, but, instead, they just showed indifference or disapproval.

When God speaks to your heart and imparts a dream to you, you will begin to face new obstacles — problems that have never before been issues in your life. But whenever discouragement begins to creep into your mind, remember what God says in Hebrews 10:36: "For ye have need of patience, that, after ye have done the will of God, ye might receive the promise."

Patience is the ability to remain steadfast and know that God's specific word to you will surely come to pass in your life. It provides the strength to continue pressing on with calm assurance and bold confidence, regardless of the adversity or the time that has transpired. Patience is an absolutely essential key to receiving a promise of God. *You will never fulfill the will of God for your life without patience.*

When you first heard from God, you may have had a tremendous passion for the dream He birthed in your heart. Initially, you may have taken a strong stance on His Word. But as you waited and *waited* — never seeing your dream manifested — you may have begun to lose your passion. Then disappointment and discouragement set in, and your fervent desire to see God's promise fulfilled in your life began to lose its intensity. Little by little, your commitment to your vision began to falter.

It's during these times of waiting, after you've done all you know to do, that you must allow patience to have its perfect work in your life (James 1:4). However, the Bible tells us that patience works with a partner. In Hebrews 6:12, the Holy Spirit exhorts us to be "...followers of them who through faith *and* patience inherit the promises." I want you to particularly notice that it says, "*through* faith and patience."

The word "through" is the Greek word *dia*, which indicates *instrumentality*. This means that our God-given dreams can only be achieved through the instrumentation of faith and patience. Or to put it another way, faith and patience are the actual instruments through which God's promises for our lives are received.

Notice that this verse doesn't exhort us to be *"followers of them who through faith, faith, and more faith received the promises."* Rather, it plainly states that we are to be "...followers of them who through faith *and* patience received the promises."

Although we must place a strong emphasis on developing faith in our lives, we need to remember that faith must be accompanied by patience. On the other hand, there are many sincere believers who are long on patience but short on faith. They could write the book on patience and waiting. But just as this verse doesn't focus solely on faith, it also doesn't say we are to follow *"them who through patience, patience, and more patience received the promises."*

Although waiting is involved in receiving your promise, this is more than just a waiting game! You must couple patience with *faith*. Patience works together with faith to defeat the dream thief of time and cause your God-given dream to come to fruition. *Both* are key instruments in experiencing the fulfillment of God's promises in your life.

> Patience works together with faith to defeat the dream thief of time and cause your God-given dream to come to fruition.

CONCEIVING AND NURTURING
GOD'S WILL FOR YOUR LIFE

By using these two words, "faith" and "patience," the Holy Spirit evokes a strong image in Hebrews 6:12. He is telling us it takes both of these virtues working together to bring our God-given dreams to fruition. Just as a husband and wife must come together to produce a child, faith and patience must come together to produce the promises of God. We can't operate in one without the other and expect to receive the fulfillment of what He has spoken to our hearts.

Let's take this analogy further. Hebrews 11:1 states, "Now faith is...." This means faith comes immediately — it takes place *now*.

The moment you choose to believe God's promise and stand on His Word with your whole being, faith rises up in your heart. Through the eyes of your spirit, you can see the full manifestation of that divine dream, for faith sees the end from the beginning. This is what I mean when I say that faith is *now*.

However, consider what would happen if faith were the only factor involved in the birth of a child. In this imaginary scenario, it would be only a matter of seconds or minutes from the moment a woman conceived until she gave birth. But such a development would be devastating to the mother. Her body would undergo such drastic physical changes in such a short period of time that she would be damaged physically, mentally, and emotionally. It would be impossible for her to adjust to such a dramatic transformation so suddenly.

In spiritual terms, this is exactly what would happen to you if the dream God gave you was manifested only through faith. The moment faith for that vision rose up in your heart — *BOOM!* — your entire life would be completely different! You would be shocked and traumatized because you wouldn't have had the period of growth and maturation you needed to handle the full manifestation of your dream.

James 1:3,4 says, "Knowing this, that the trying of your faith worketh patience. But let patience have her perfect work, that ye may be perfect and entire, wanting nothing." Immediately after you receive a vision from God, the dream thieves will begin to test your faith in what He has said. That's when you quickly discover that the only way to defeat the dream thieves and hold fast to your word from Heaven is to *grow up* — and that means developing patience!

In the practical, everyday sense, patience means facing the testing of your faith fully clothed in spiritual armor, equipped with the Word of God and the power of the Holy Spirit. (*See* my book, *Dressed To Kill*, to read an in-depth description of spiritual armor.) If you'll put on the full armor of God each day and allow the testing of your faith to work patience in your life, you'll defeat the dream thieves *and* reach a new level of maturity. You'll "...be perfect and entire, wanting nothing" — which is a blessed way to be!

Patience brings God's perfect timing into the picture, for without patience, there can be no "due season." In other words, patience enables us to endure the period of waiting between the promise and the fulfillment — the "due season" when our dreams come to pass at exactly the right time.

In His infinite wisdom, God knows that we need time to adjust to the changes in our lives that will result from the fulfillment of our vision. Therefore, He included patience, or "hang-in-there power," as one of the fruits of the Spirit available to us. Patience allows the Holy Spirit to make the necessary adjustments in our lives to accommodate our dream. It is the sustaining force in our spirit man that builds up our "faith muscle." And as it strengthens our faith, patience simultaneously brings forth perfection and maturity in our lives.

> Patience enables us to endure the period of waiting between the promise and the fulfillment — the "due season" when our dreams come to pass at exactly the right time.

The process of walking in faith and patience is very similar to that of having a baby. In the beginning, it's always very exciting to conceive a word of God in your heart. You get to share the great news with friends and relatives and tell everyone at your church about your new dream. But as you begin to walk out that dream day by day, it's easy to develop "morning sickness"!

During this time of waiting, the manifestation of your vision can seem distant and unattainable, and you may even feel sorry you ever heard from God. But even if you seem stuck in the middle, there is no turning back. That dream *will* come forth if you will just hold fast with patience to your faith!

With the passing of time, your dream will continue to grow bigger until it seems like it will explode inside you. As the manifestation of your vision draws near, you may feel as if your life is changing radically and moving too fast. In fact, you may actually feel incredible pain prior to the full realization of your dream.

It's just a fact that you will be required to make major adjustments in your life to see the fulfillment of the vision God has given you. You will have to discard wrong attitudes and stretch in ways you never knew were possible. When that happens, all you'll be able to think about is getting that "baby" out!

But you'll have to continue to wait in faith and patience for that dream from the Lord to manifest. Meanwhile, God will work on your bad attitudes, your negative actions and reactions, and the wrong motivations in your heart. Remember, He doesn't want to just use you or bless you; He wants to *change* you in the process.

Then, finally, the moment will come, and the goal you've dreamed of and persevered for will burst forth into the natural realm. What you imagined deep in your spirit for months or even years, you will suddenly see, touch, and hold in your hands. Faith and patience will be the proud new parents of a miracle in your life!

This is precisely why Paul wrote, "And let us not be weary in well doing: for in due season we shall reap, if we faint not" (Galatians 6:9). Time has a way of wearing down our resistance, but the Bible urges us to stay on track and stick with the vision in our hearts. We may have to wait, but that's all right! Our dream must be nurtured until the proper time of delivery. Although it may take much more time than we may have anticipated, we *shall* reap in due season "if we faint not."

You may be thinking, *I'm tired of waiting, and I'm about to give up. Does that mean I'm "fainting?" If I stop right now, will it jeopardize what God wants to do in my life?*

The word "faint" in this verse is the Greek word *ekluomai*, which is a compound of *ek* and *luo*. The word *ek* simply means *out*, and *luo* means *to loose* or *to loosen*. When these two words are compounded together, the new word depicts *a person who is utterly exhausted and worn out to the point of giving up*. One might say that this individual is so weary that he has become undone and unraveled and has simply given up hope of ever seeing a change in his life.

Never allow the dream thieves to push you to the brink of giving up. Rather than let pressures build to the point of breaking you, you must learn how to throw your cares and concerns upon the Lord and then determine to *leave* them in His loving hands. As First Peter 5:7 instructs, "Casting *all* your care upon him; for he careth for you."

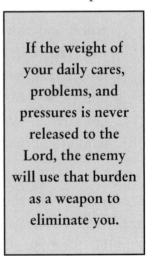

If the weight of your daily cares, problems, and pressures is never released to the Lord, the enemy will use that burden as a weapon to eliminate you.

If the weight of your daily cares, problems, and pressures is never released to the Lord, the enemy will use that burden as a weapon to eliminate you. You can become so utterly exhausted and worn down as you try to carry your dream on your own that you simply give up on the vision in your heart. That's why you must never forget that the battle is not yours, but the Lord's (*see* 2 Chronicles 20:15)!

Achieving God's plan for your life will take time, for your dream must be cultivated and nurtured. However, if you hold tightly to the word God has placed in your heart and cast all your cares upon Him, you will not faint, and your due season *will* come. Nearly everything that is valuable and worthwhile takes time to produce, and there is nothing more fulfilling than watching faith and patience bring forth a miracle in your life!

Can You Delay Your Destiny?

Habakkuk 2:2-4 is particularly pertinent to this subject of a God-given vision being fulfilled in "due season":

> **And the Lord answered me, and said, Write the vision, and make it plain upon tables, that he may run that readeth it. For the vision is yet for an appointed time, but at the end it shall speak, and not lie: though it tarry, wait for it; because it will surely come, it will not tarry. Behold, his soul which is lifted up is not upright in him: but the just shall live by his faith.**

Sometimes the plan of God for our lives is delayed — not because of the devil, but because of *us*! This passage tells us that once we're absolutely sure we've heard from God, we must "run" with the vision He placed in our hearts.

Unfortunately, this is where many believers make a critical mistake. Instead of taking steps to run with their dream, they erroneously assume it will come to pass simply because God spoke it to them. Although they wait and wait for something to happen, nothing will ever happen until they change their way of thinking! They're merely hoping for "pie in the sky" — something grand and glorious that requires zero effort on their part. Yet no matter how long they sit and twiddle their thumbs, their dream will never come to pass.

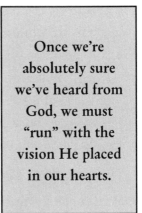

Once we're absolutely sure we've heard from God, we must "run" with the vision He placed in our hearts.

Then when their promise isn't fulfilled, these believers often blame their failure on a demonic attack coming against them to abort the plan of God for their lives. Yet even though Satan will certainly try to attack them and thwart their dream, this usually isn't the primary reason why people fail to realize their potential. If the issue was just a demonic assault, they could eradicate it with prayer, the Word, the anointing, and spiritual warfare — because God's Word always works!

However, when people sit around meditating on unrealistic notions — waiting for that special "break" that will thrust their careers ahead or give them the upper edge — they may as well go ahead and kiss their dream good-bye. As they say in good ol' Southern slang, "Folks, it just ain't gonna happen!" If a person truly wants to see the vision in his heart fulfilled, it will require some serious elbow grease and hard work on his part.

This principle is evident in God's promise to give the land of Canaan to the children of Israel. He told them, "Every place that the sole of your foot shall tread upon, that have I given unto you..." (Joshua 1:3). In other words, God was declaring, *"I'm giving you that land, but for you to possess it, you must get up and aggressively go after it! If you'll put your foot on the land I have promised you and take charge, it will be yours!"*

If the nation of Israel had just sat in the wilderness and looked at the Promised Land from afar, wondering when it would miraculously drop into their laps, they never would have received their rightful inheritance. For the Promised Land to be theirs, the Israelites had to obey God, jerk the slack and unbelief out of their lives, and *go take the land*! If they would aggressively pursue His plan, God promised that He'd make sure they succeeded in their endeavor.

Likewise, when Jesus charged the Church with the Great Commission, He didn't say, "I'm giving you the whole world, and you don't have to do anything!" He called believers to *action*, saying, "Go ye therefore, and *teach* all nations, *baptizing* them in the name of the Father, and of the Son, and of the Holy Ghost: *teaching* them to observe all things whatsoever I have commanded you..." (Matthew 28:19,20).

To "take the world" for Jesus, we must move out of our comfort zones and actively strive to reach the lost with the message of the Gospel. We must preach and teach with fire and passion, and then we must baptize new converts to begin the process of discipleship in their lives. In other words, we can take this world for Jesus *if* we will put some perspiration and effort into what

God has called us to do. The fulfillment of our vision is not going to just drop out of Heaven!

This is exactly what Jesus meant when He said, "...The kingdom of heaven suffereth violence, and the violent take it by force" (Matthew 11:12). If we're going to reach the entire world with the Gospel during our generation, we must develop an aggressive, forceful mentality. We must mentally gear up, surrender to the power of the Spirit, crucify the flesh, and then *pursue our God-given dream with all our hearts and our strength*!

When God speaks to our hearts and gives us a word for our lives, we need to get up and *run* with it. When we do nothing to prepare for or move toward the promise God has given us, we can delay or thwart His plan for us for years or even for decades.

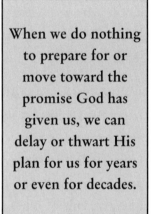

When we do nothing to prepare for or move toward the promise God has given us, we can delay or thwart His plan for us for years or even for decades.

Countless believers have told me, "God spoke to my heart and told me that I'm going to be a millionaire. I'm going to be a tremendous giver to the Body of Christ in these last days." Yet many of these are lazy individuals who don't have a single "get-up-and-go" bone in their bodies! They never strive to get a better job — or if they do, they refuse to do the necessary work to fulfill their vision and excel in it. They never learn how to budget their finances or how to be good stewards over what they already have.

Even though these believers may have sincerely tapped into God's ultimate plan for their lives, they will never see that plan realized unless they make major changes in the way they think and live. They will not just wake up one day and discover that they're millionaires. That kind of fairy-tale mentality is an unrealistic view of Christianity and never bears fruit.

On the other hand, I also know people who have heard from God and are aggressively pursuing the dreams He placed in their hearts. These believers aren't waiting for God to do it all; they're taking action. For instance, I personally know several men and women who have been called as givers and who pursue their calling with every fiber of their being. They are hardworking people who are constantly finding ways to make more money so they can sow it into the work of God's Kingdom both in their own nation and in missions worldwide.

I've observed how these wonderful believers live. Rather than idly sitting by and waiting for divine, sovereign financial miracles to float into their lives to make them instantly rich, they develop businesses, plan investments, and so on. Furthermore, they don't wait for the big bucks before they start giving — they give out of what they have and believe God for increase so they can give more!

These are people God can bless! Through their active obedience, they prove their sincerity and their commitment to His plan for their lives. They are being positioned, *by their own actions*, to fulfill the dreams God has planted in their hearts.

I wonder how many Christians have blamed the devil for the lack of fruit in their lives, when they themselves are their own biggest enemy. Now, please don't misinterpret what I'm saying. I know that there is a real devil and that he will do everything he can to overthrow God's plan for a person's life. I have had to deal with many such attacks in my own life and ministry.

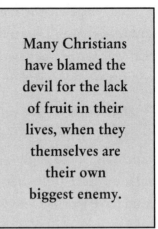

Many Christians have blamed the devil for the lack of fruit in their lives, when they themselves are their own biggest enemy.

However, in many cases the devil never even gets a chance to eliminate a believer from his or her race. Believers — called of God before the foundations of the earth and anointed by Him to fulfill specific assignments — often eliminate themselves by doing nothing with their divine calling. They either abort God's plan themselves by being lazy and half-hearted about what He has told them to do, or they don't spend enough time with Him to even discover the purpose He has put them on this earth to fulfill. This complacent mindset serves only to play into the enemy's hands and has no place in the Kingdom of God.

If you want your God-given dream to come to pass right on time, you must do your part and *take action*! Begin to make the preparations needed to fulfill that divine assignment. If God told you that you're called to funnel money into the preaching of the Gospel, it's up to you to study everything you can in the Word about prosperity and finances and to start putting what the Holy Spirit reveals into practice. If He has called you to teach His Word, dig into the Bible and study. Go to Bible school, if God leads you in that direction, and then teach anywhere people will listen.

It's true that there is a "due season" to every divine purpose and that we can't hasten God's perfect timing. But it is also true that our wrong behavior — and that can be as simple as *doing nothing* — can certainly *delay* His timing.

People often ask me, "Rick, how has the Lord been able to do so much through your ministry over the years?" Many are expecting some super-spiritual answer, so you can imagine how deflated they feel when I reply, "Because Denise and I and our team have worked very, very hard over the past years to do what God told us to do."

Some people even give me an offended look as if to tell me, "How dare you say that your ministry has succeeded because of you and your hard work! You glory-stealer! Don't you know that it's all because of God! It's not because of your hard work, Renner! It's because of the anointing! How dare you attribute the blessing of God to your hard work!"

Of course, I know that the blessing and anointing of God has played a primary role in our ministry. But what if Denise and I had never done anything — never worked, prayed, taught, studied, planned, or taken steps to begin implementing the dream God had planted in our hearts? Do you know where we'd be today? We'd be sitting at home, depressed because we had no sense of purpose or direction for our lives and wondering why everyone else seemed to be moving ahead while we stagnated, stuck in the same old place we'd always been.

James 2:26 tells us, "For as the body without the spirit is dead, so faith without works is dead also." God blesses our faith, and faith is always expressed in works. If we're doing all we know to do — exercising our faith by working as the Holy Spirit directs and leads us — patience will easily be developed in our lives. On the other hand, staying idle while dwelling on fantasies breeds impatience, and impatience cultivates a bitter, unthankful attitude — another sinister obstacle to the fulfillment of our dreams.

Patience is often just a matter of standing firm after you've done all you know to do. It also involves continuing to do what God is leading you to do on a daily basis.

So don't delay your dream by refusing to recognize that you have a vital role to play in seeing it all come to pass. Once you accept that fact, let the Word of God and the Holy Spirit direct and enable you to pursue your dream one day at a time by doing *your* part. You can never know too much of God's Word, become too saturated by His Spirit, or prepare too much for a miracle!

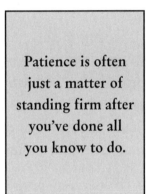

Patience is often just a matter of standing firm after you've done all you know to do.

AN APPOINTED TIME

When you first receive a word from the Lord, it's tremendously exciting! You want to "shout it from the rooftops" and let the whole world know! But then another desire begins welling up within you — a strong, intense desire to know *when* this magnificent vision is going to come to pass.

This is where we often get into trouble. In our anxious state, we may even try to project the specific time our dream will come to fruition. We take on the role of self-appointed prognosticators without actually knowing what we're doing.

Remember, Habakkuk 2:3 tells us, "For the vision is *yet for an appointed time*...." This statement usually takes the wind right out of our sails, because we come face to face with the hard reality that the great dream God gave us isn't going to happen overnight. It will come to pass only according to *God's* timing, not according to ours.

Living in this "microwave culture" of instant gratification, we often expect everything to be fast and easy. We receive a promise of God with great excitement and burst out of the prayer closet with great expectations and grand plans — only to bump into the wall of "an appointed time." This is *the patience zone*, an essential dimension of the Christian life.

Too often people make sweeping statements about what they'll accomplish for God. But when their vision doesn't manifest as quickly as they expected, they become discouraged and begin to let go of the dream.

But the truth is, each believer must wait to see his word from God come to pass at its appointed time. If a person decides in his own mind the time frame in which his word from God will manifest in his life, he sets himself up for certain disappointment.

Let me warn you: If God doesn't give you a date for the manifestation of your dream or specifically tell you to set a date, don't do it! When you set a date — and then you watch that day arrive without anything being accomplished — it's extremely disappointing. It can also be quite embarrassing, especially if you told a lot of other people about the date you had set. Sadly, many believers have let go of their dreams simply because they were embarrassed when the self-appointed date came and went without the results they were hoping for.

Although we usually groan at the mention of patience, this godly character trait gives us victory over discouragement and prevents embarrassment. It enables us to hold fast to our dream until God's promise in Habakkuk 2:3 is fulfilled: "For the vision is yet for an appointed time, but at the end it shall speak, and not lie: though it tarry, wait for it; because it will surely come, it will not tarry."

HE IS FAITHFUL

While waiting on the fulfillment of our dreams, we may start feeling exhausted, or we may even be tempted to think God lied to us. But that's the time we must determine to *hold fast* to our word from the Lord. The Bible promises that, if we will wait in faith, "...it will *surely* come...."

Let's look at Hebrews 10:23 again. It says, "Let us hold fast the profession of our faith without wavering; (for he is faithful that promised;)..." The Greek word for "wavering" is *klino*, which means *to bow down, to slope the shoulders, to bend over,* or *to go to bed*. It can also be translated "couch." For example, this word is used in Matthew 9:2,6 to describe the man who was sick of the palsy, lying on a couch. By using this particular word, this verse is saying in essence, *"Hold fast the profession of your faith, for if you let go of that dream, you will lose your sense of purpose in this life and will end up going to bed on your faith!"*

The real reason people give up hope and quit believing is that they don't really believe "He is faithful that promised." They might say, "But I've waited and waited, and God hasn't done anything I thought He was going to do! Oh, I've seen others blessed — I've watched them shout with joy as their prayers were answered. But not my prayers! They're still the same old unanswered prayers. I'm sick of it all, and I'm not going to believe and wait for God to come through any longer. Forget it — I'm letting it all go!"

> The real reason people give up hope and quit believing is that they don't really believe "He is faithful that promised."

If you have this mindset, I suggest that you meditate on Habakkuk 2:4, which says, "Behold, his soul which is lifted up is not upright in him: but the just shall live by his faith." As you wait for your vision to come to pass, your soul can be tempted to rise up and question the integrity of God Himself. But when that happens, you inevitably begin to confess doubt and unbelief. And if you doubt God's faithfulness — if you allow your soul to be "lifted up" within you against the word He has spoken to you — your dream will not be realized.

By declaring "...the just shall live by his faith," the Holy Spirit is reminding you that you must constantly live by faith if you are to see your vision manifested in your life. Having patience means that you don't stop believing — *no matter what your flesh or your soul tries to bring against the Word*!

The writer of Hebrews declared that God is faithful, and all the heroes of faith in the Old and New Testaments knew this to be so. Regardless of how many times they messed up as they pursued the plan of God, these godly men and women saw His promises fulfilled in their lives because they persevered in faith and maintained their fire for the Lord.

Many scriptures extol and proclaim the faithfulness of God. For instance, Romans 4:20 states that Abraham "...staggered not at the promise of God through unbelief; but was strong in faith..." because he was "...*fully persuaded* that, what he [God] had promised, he was able also to perform" (v. 21).

Paul also speaks of his confidence in the Lord's faithfulness in Philippians 1:6, saying, "Being confident of this very thing, that he which hath begun a good work in you will perform it until the day of Jesus Christ...." And in Second Timothy 2:13, Paul makes an astonishing statement: "If we believe not, yet he abideth faithful: he cannot deny himself."

At the core of God's being is faithfulness. God performs what He promises because it is His nature to do so. He cannot deny Himself, for He is faithful. But you must *choose to believe* that He will do what He has promised. You must set your heart and commit your will, making an irrevocable decision to believe God's Word, regardless of how you feel, what you think, what others say, or how your circumstances look.

I hear many believers say, "I know God said that this is what He wants for my life, but I just find it so hard to believe." Of course it's hard to believe! The natural mind can't fully comprehend the things of God (1 Corinthians 2:14). That's why believers have to renew their minds with God's Word, training their minds to think the way He thinks (Romans 12:2).

> You must set your heart and commit your will, making an irrevocable decision to believe God's Word regardless of how you feel, what you think, what others say, or how your circumstances look.

You see, patience isn't passive. It's an aggressive decision to meditate on and to believe what God has spoken — even when the dream thieves assail you and try to steal your vision. Patience deliberately *chooses* to believe that God is faithful.

CALL TO REMEMBRANCE

Hebrews 10:32 tells us what to do when we become discouraged or are tempted to doubt God's faithfulness. It says, "But *call to remembrance the former days....*"

For the Hebrew believers to whom this epistle was written, the memories of the strong faith and the awesome miracles they had experienced in the early days had been clouded over as year after difficult year had passed by. These believers had waited and waited for their dreams to be fulfilled and for God's promises to manifest in their lives, but so far nothing had happened except trouble, hardship, and a great deal of loss. Certainly they had experienced God's power, but they had also suffered through many struggles as the enemy did his best to destroy their faith.

Disappointment had set in. The hearts of these Hebrew believers were growing weary, and they were beginning to think it was all just a terrible farce. Yet even as the winds of adversity sought to extinguish the flickering flame of their dreams, the Holy Spirit urged them to "...call to remembrance the former days...."

During periods of frustration and doubt such as these Hebrew believers were experiencing, the Bible instructs us to put everything on hold, silence our minds, still our emotions, and *remember*. We are to let our minds drift back to our early experiences with the Lord when our faith was simple, uncomplicated, and childlike.

Do you remember those days?

- Can you remember moments when you were wondrously filled with the Holy Spirit?

- Can you recall times when you experienced God's supernatural power and received direct answers to prayer as you prayed in the name of Jesus?

- Can you remember the "former days" when you first knew you had the power to witness to your friends and family?

- Do you recall how you burned with a spiritual passion to see your loved ones saved?

- Do you remember what it was like to view your Bible in a fresh, precious way and to carry it nearly everywhere you went?

Hebrews 10:32 teaches us to call these early spiritual experiences to remembrance. In other words, when our minds and bodies are ready to quit because the dream we're believing for is still unfulfilled, we must consciously decide to remember God's faithfulness to us and how we felt when we first received His direction for our lives.

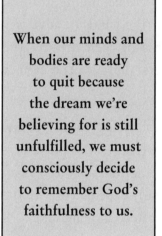

When our minds and bodies are ready to quit because the dream we're believing for is still unfulfilled, we must consciously decide to remember God's faithfulness to us.

If we're discouraged and feeling defeated, our flesh won't want to remember such times. Thus, we must actively make an effort to think upon our experiences of intimacy and victory with the Lord. We must actively "call them to remembrance." If we fail to take the initiative to do this, we *won't* remember. We can only bring the former days to remembrance as we *choose* to do it!

In Hebrews 10:32, the phrase "call to remembrance" could be translated *to recollect*. It carries the idea of *looking into the past and digging up hard-to-find, good memories*. You see, bad memories are easily remembered, and the flesh loves to hang on to them. Good memories, however, are often quickly forgotten and overshadowed by negative circumstances that can loom over us, blocking out the light of truth.

Thus, this verse carries the idea, *"There are some memories that you must not bury! Go back and pull them out of the past, and erect them as monuments to God's faithfulness in your life. They should always be in the forefront of your mind."*

Whenever you become discouraged and your faith begins to waver, your flesh tries to make you think, *This situation is hopeless, and I'm a failure. The dream I've been pursuing was just my own fantasy. I should just give up and be like everyone else.* In such times, you must make a decision to "call to remembrance the former days" — those great monuments of victory in your past. It will take a committed decision and some concerted effort to push aside the flesh, shove discouragement out of the way, and dig into the recesses of your mind to bring your memories of God's faithfulness to the forefront of your thinking. The process isn't always easy — but it's what God requires.

Follow David's example when he faced Goliath: Square your shoulders, stand tall, and march toward your giant — confidently declaring that God will deliver you from any pressure or obstacle that seeks to destroy your God-given dream. Subdue your flesh by praising God and thanking Him for bringing you through every challenging circumstance.

ILLUMINATION

Hebrews 10:32 continues, "But call to remembrance the former days, *in which, after ye were illuminated....*" The Greek word for "illuminated" is *photizo*, which refers to *a brilliant flash of light.* The word "photography" is derived from this Greek word, depicting the blinding flash of a camera.

Do you remember the first time the Word of God shot through your being like a bolt of lightning, revealing truth to you and bringing order to the chaos in your life? Do you remember when God first imparted the dream of greatness for your life to your heart?

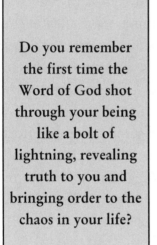

> Do you remember the first time the Word of God shot through your being like a bolt of lightning, revealing truth to you and bringing order to the chaos in your life?

Satan doesn't want you to fulfill God's plan for your life; in fact, he has his *own* purpose for you. That's why it's so important to understand this: If you don't walk in the path God has set before you — if you reject His plan for your life — you can be sure that the devil is ready and waiting to put *his* plan for your life into action. Therefore, your God-given vision must be an illumination in your life to which you can always return. Your revelation must shine so brilliantly in your heart and mind that it lights your way through any darkness the enemy tries to bring against you.

I vividly remember when the Lord first called me into the ministry. He gave me a *photizo* — an illumination that lit up my heart — and the light of that vision has given me strength and courage to persevere through every difficult situation and to seek victory from every back-stabbing attack.

You see, I *know* God spoke to me; I *know* He called me. I *know* that the things He showed me will happen in my life. And the words the Lord imparted to me when He first called me remain a torch of truth in my soul, giving me steadfast patience as I study His Word and seek Him for wisdom in fulfilling what He has ordained for my life. As Psalm 119:105 says, God's words to me are a "…lamp unto my feet, and a light unto my path."

Think of the heroes of faith listed in Hebrews 11. Why were these men and women able to travel across deserts with their families, living in tents as "strangers and pilgrims on the earth" (v. 13)? Because they had been illuminated! How were they able to bear the ridicule and scorn, the hardships and the difficulties? Because they had been illuminated!

REJOICING IN AFFLICTION

Remembrance and illumination sustain patience — but something unexpected always follows, which you must be prepared to handle. Hebrews 10:32 continues, "But call to remembrance the former days, in which, after ye were illuminated, *ye endured a great fight of afflictions*.…"

As you dash out of the prayer closet with your word from God and collide with "the patience zone," you'll also become entangled in the wrestling match of your life. Just because God spoke to you about your business, talent, or career, that doesn't mean the dream He planted in your heart will burst onto the scene without resistance or adversity. You'll have to fight a few battles before the vision you see with the eyes of your spirit becomes visible to the natural eye.

In verse 32, the Greek word for "fight" refers to *combat in the public arena*. I want to stress the idea of "public" here because almost every "fight of affliction" in your life will be a public spectacle. Hebrews 10:33 says, "Partly, whilst ye were made a *gazingstock* both by reproaches and afflictions; and partly, whilst ye became companions of them that were so used."

> You'll have to fight a few battles before the vision you see with the eyes of your spirit becomes visible to the natural eye.

Once a believer hears from Heaven and steps out to obey the vision God has given him, that person is usually thrust in the public arena. Rarely do people have a private fight of faith as they carry out God's plan for their lives.

The moment the Holy Spirit supernaturally speaks a word of guidance to you, that's when you begin to move out of the spectators' seats and onto the stage. You may become a prime subject of conversation with your friends and family as everyone tries to determine whether or not you will make it.

Ironically, if you dropped your dream and never took a stance of faith, no one would ever say anything about you. But as soon as you declare, "God called me to do this," people's tongues begin to wag furiously as they discuss whether they're witnessing a terrible joke or a miracle in the making.

The fight that ensues — the "fight of afflictions" — is an emotional one. The Greek word for "afflictions" in verse 32 is *pathos*, which can refer to *emotional suffering*. The most traumatic battles are fought in the realm of the soul, where your emotions can swallow you in a sea of fear, grief, or rage in the matter of a split second if they are not brought under the discipline of the Holy Spirit.

As I said before, you will have to deal with challenges you've never experienced before when you recognize the divine course God has set before you and begin to walk it out. Family members who were very supportive in the past may now doubt your ability to discern the leading of the Holy Spirit. Some may even doubt your sanity! Many may tell you repeatedly that they believe you're going to fall flat on your face. A few may even secretly hope to see it happen.

It's during these intense periods of emotional pain that patience becomes *endurance*. Endurance is not just the ability to trudge on through the quagmire of life. *Endurance is choosing to rejoice in the midst of the affliction of emotional suffering.*

In First Peter 4:12 and 13, Peter exhorts us not to be surprised or shocked when such difficult times arise. In fact, we are to rejoice in them!

> **Beloved, think it not strange concerning the fiery trial which is to try you, as though some strange thing happened unto you: But rejoice, inasmuch as ye are partakers of Christ's sufferings; that, when his glory shall be revealed, ye may be glad also with exceeding joy.**

You're probably asking, "How in the world can I rejoice when my friends think I'm crazy, my family is ashamed of me, and I've become the object of public ridicule — all because I'm standing on this word I received from God?"

Hebrews 12:2 tells us how to rejoice in affliction, giving Jesus as our ultimate Example: "Looking unto Jesus the author and finisher of our faith; who *for the joy that was set before him endured the cross*...." In *His* time of affliction, Jesus was illuminated with the promise of our salvation to come and the great exploits of faith and mighty victories we would bring forth through His name.

> Jesus endured His great fight of afflictions, sustained patience, and never lost faith that God's promise would come to pass.

Jesus endured His great fight of afflictions, sustained patience, and never lost faith that God's promise would come to pass. Jesus' entire being was illuminated with the revelation that after the Cross would come the resurrection — and that once He was seated at the right hand of the Father, the Church would come forth on the earth to storm the gates of hell!

Let me clarify that I'm not advocating emotional suffering, and I certainly don't enjoy suffering myself. But the Word of God teaches us that *we must determine in our hearts to hold fast to our dreams, regardless of the obstacles, persecutions, or afflictions we encounter.* The apostle Peter explains the outcome of that all-important decision in First Peter 5:10: "But the God of all grace, who hath called us unto his eternal glory by Christ Jesus, after that ye have suffered a while, *make you perfect, stablish, strengthen, settle you.*"

You have to make that determination at the very birth of a dream in your heart, because your emotions soar when God first gives you a vision. The enemy knows this. He also knows that the higher your emotions rise, the harder they can fall. Satan will therefore do everything in his power to cause you to come crashing back down to earth in failure. However, if your "day of illumination" remains vividly real to you — if you choose to remember your past victories and to rejoice in the face of challenges that cause emotional upheaval — the devil has absolutely no power over your life.

To see your dream accomplished, you'll eventually have to dig in your heels and say, "I'm going to stay right here and respond only to what God promised. He called me to do this, and I'm going to stand firm and do it. I don't care how heavy the load gets, how hot the fire of opposition blazes around me, or how dark the sky appears. I'm holding fast to my God-given dream, and I won't budge until I see it come to pass! *And* I'm going to praise and worship God through it all, no matter what comes my way!"

That is patience. That is endurance. That is perseverance. That is *illumination* that results in a life of fulfillment and rejoicing. When you choose to respond this way as you pursue your dream, you release the rock-solid, bold confidence that God imparts with His Word. This is absolutely the way you have to live in order to accomplish the will of God for your life.

Think About It

Dreams are conceived by faith in an instant, but it takes time for a dream to come to pass. Faith held steady by patience will prevent time from becoming a dream thief in your life. Time provides the opportunity for growth and maturity to take place. When you keep faith *and* patience tightly joined in your life, you will emerge through the passage of time "perfect and entire" (James 1:4), equipped to walk out the fullness of your dream.

If you work *with* time, it won't work *against* you. How are you working with time to take advantage of opportunities to prepare for your dream to come to pass in its fullness?

When it comes to making your dream happen, you can't do God's part, and He won't do yours. If you want your dream to come to pass in due season, you have to do your part by taking steps to move in the direction of its fulfillment.

What has God told you to do? Have you developed daily habits to keep you moving steadily toward that dream? If you have lost your sense of purpose, it is because you have stopped *pursuing* your purpose. Reignite your faith by reminding yourself of the dream God gave you, and then take action that propels you in the direction of that goal.

Idleness and fantasy-thinking breed impatience and contempt. Such patterns will pull you into the miry pit of bitterness and ingratitude — which is the slippery descent that ultimately leads to spiritual complacency. Think of three things you can do to express your gratitude for what God has done for you and to revive your passion for what He has prepared for you.

The fight of faith is part of the process you must experience in order to develop the spiritual stamina you need to stand strong and walk in your God-given dream. If you are facing various difficulties, count it all joy — knowing that as you stay in faith, walk in love, and stand in patience, the person you'll become through the fight is the person you need to be in order to occupy your God-given promise.

Take a quick survey of your present difficulties — and then rejoice! God's grace is greater than any challenge you may face!

CHAPTER SEVEN

WHAT TO DO WHEN
YOU RECEIVE GOD'S CALL

*T*he call of God rarely comes at a convenient moment. Rather, it usually comes when you are in the middle of doing something else or when you've already made other plans. Then suddenly God speaks to your heart, and you are jarred into facing the reality that He is asking you to do something you hadn't previously considered or thought about. From that moment forward, you start trying to figure out how to get from where you are to where you need to be in order to accomplish what God is asking you to do!

For instance, you might wonder:

- *What about the house payments?*

- *What about my job?*

- *What about all my current commitments?*

- *What about my credit-card debt and the bills I need to pay?*

- *What about my relationships? How will this decision affect those around me?*

- *What about my parents? How will God's call on my life change my availability to them?*

These are usually the questions that arise in your mind when the reality of God's call begins to dawn on you. At that point, you need to know what steps to take next. How do you release yourself from your current commitments so you can follow the dream God has put in your heart?

> When the reality of God's call begins to dawn on you, you need to know what steps to take next. How do you release yourself from your current commitments so you can follow the dream God has put in your heart?

If I've just described some of the questions you're asking right now, you're not alone. The truth is, you have just joined the ranks of other men and women of God in "The Hall of Faith" who were also quite jarred and shocked when the call of God came to them!

Certainly that was true in the case of Noah, Abraham, and Moses, as we read in previous chapters. It was also true in the prophet Elisha's case, whose story represents one of the greatest scriptural examples of the call of God coming to a person. The account is found in First Kings 19:19-21, where we read how God used Elijah to call Elisha into the ministry. Verse 19 says, "So he [Elijah] departed thence, and found Elisha the son of Shaphat, who was plowing with twelve yoke of oxen before him, and he with the twelfth: and Elijah passed by him, and cast his mantle upon him."

Elisha became the disciple and assistant of Elijah, the great and dramatic prophet of God. Elisha followed Elijah patiently, waiting for the moment when Elijah's prophetic mantle would pass to him and he would become the inheritor of a mighty anointing. At last the day came when Elijah was taken up into Heaven in a chariot of fire. As that chariot carried him up into the heavens, his mantle dropped from the sky and fell to Elisha.

However, let's back up for a moment to see how all this first began with Elisha.

When the prophet Elijah first found Elisha, he was just a simple farmer, busy doing what he had been doing for years — plowing the fields with his team of oxen. I'm sure Elisha must have deeply loved God and served Him faithfully; otherwise, God wouldn't have called him into the ministry. But at that moment, Elisha wasn't in the prayer closet seeking God's will for his life. It seems he was just working at his job, doing what he knew to do, when *suddenly* the call of God came to him.

When God asks a person to do something he has never done before, it's natural for him to wonder if he's equipped to do the job. It's normal for the mind to ask, *Has God chosen the right person for this job?* Millions of people have asked these same questions — *including me!* But the primary reason people don't step out and obey what God is telling them to do is that they are afraid to take that big leap of faith.

It seems like every time Denise and I and our ministry team get settled in a routine and feel confident about what we're doing, God puts something additional on our plate. That should be true with all of us. You see, when we've proven ourselves faithful and successful at what we're doing right now, this reveals to God that we're ready for the next level of responsibility and promotion.

> The primary reason people don't step out and obey what God is telling them to do is that they are afraid to take that big leap of faith.

Now let me walk you through the story of Elisha so you can see the kind of person God desires to use. I think you'll be encouraged, strengthened, and blessed when you realize you are *exactly* that kind of person!

GOD CALLED SOMEONE WHO WAS ALREADY FAITHFUL IN WHAT HE WAS DOING

When the call came to Elisha, he was already very busy in life. His occupation was clearly defined, and he had become very good at what he was doing. In fact, the Bible tells us that Elisha was so committed to his business, he was *yoked* to his team of oxen. This is symbolic of the state his life was in at the time.

Notice that the Bible is also careful to mention that Elisha had 12 yoke, or 12 pairs, of oxen. In biblical times, oxen were very expensive. They were the tractors and plows of that day.

Very few farmers were wealthy enough to own 24 oxen, which is why the Bible so plainly tells us that Elisha owned that many. Those oxen represented *very big money*!

This tells us that Elisha was no small-time farmer. To own 12 yoke of oxen, he must have been huge in the farming business!

If a person is going to do well in any business, he has to be well-connected and financially stable. He must also possess the common sense needed to run a business. Therefore, the fact that Elisha owned 12 yoke of oxen reveals that he was a good businessman. We can also assume that he had many friends in the business. I'm sure he bought, sold, and traded with people throughout the entire area where he lived. His business was successful and prospering.

However, having a successful business doesn't happen by accident. It takes hard work, undivided attention, and lots of time. That means Elisha was successful because he did what was necessary to be blessed. He was very good and very faithful in his occupation.

There are several important things we can learn from this fact. *Listen very carefully, because many people don't understand what I am about to tell you — and that's why they are unsuccessful in their lives, businesses, and ministries.*

As we discussed in the last chapter, people often get the impression that God calls those who are just sitting around waiting for something to happen. They have a "pie in the sky" mentality. They think that one day out of the clear blue, a lightning bolt is going to strike them from Heaven. Suddenly their lives will change, and they will be catapulted into a fabulous, phenomenal life! But these people are relying on a very wrong impression that borders on being hallucinatory.

When I read and study my Bible, I can't find one person significantly used by God who was lazily doing nothing when His call came to him or her. Just as is true in the case of Elisha, all the men and women of God written about in Scripture were already busy doing something when the Lord spoke to them.

Think about it — why would God want to call someone to do *His* work when that person hasn't successfully done his or her own work?

PRODUCTIVITY IS IMPORTANT TO GOD

God likes to associate with people who know how to work. We see this in Jesus' parable in Matthew 25:14-30, where He taught about the master who gave talents to three of his servants. Jesus said when that master returned from a long trip, he expected to see *increase* and *productivity* as a result of what he'd previously given to his servants. The two servants who proved faithful and worked hard were richly rewarded. But Jesus let us know that the servant who did *nothing* was "unprofitable" (the Greek word *achreios* literally means *useless* or *good for nothing*).

In this parable, Jesus taught that faithfulness and hard work is commendable in the Kingdom of God. *He also taught that*

WHAT TO DO WHEN YOU RECEIVE GOD'S CALL

those who dream about being promoted need to get busy using what they have right now. This tells us that Jesus appreciates hardworking, faithful, "use-what-they-have" people. (For a more in-depth study of this vital principle, *see* Chapter 3 of my book, *If You Were God, Would You Choose You?*)

> Those who dream about being promoted need to get busy using what they have right now.

God is also impressed by people who handle money well. I hear people say, "Oh, God, give me Your power so I can touch the nations!" But one of the most basic tests God uses to determine how much spiritual power He will give a person is to see how he or she handles money.

Money is a form of power; however, it is the *lowest* form. With money, you can do a lot of things. But if you don't appreciate the value and power of money — which is a natural, low form of power — why would God trust you with His spiritual, supernatural power?

"Super-spiritual" people tend to overlook these considerations, but God does not. When God needs someone to do something for Him, He looks for someone who has already demonstrated he or she knows how to handle money, knows how to work, and knows how to stick with the job until it's done!

My experience has shown me that most lazy people spend a lot of time fantasizing. They dream about their future. They dream about the day they will have more money. They dream about having a big ministry. But this kind of dreaming is nothing

> Hard work and learning to be responsible are essential qualities for any person who is going to do something big in life.

more than *escapism* from reality! These people need to quit dreaming and get to work! *Hard work and learning to be responsible are essential qualities for any person who is going to do something big in life.*

It's obvious from what I've already said in this book that I believe in God-given dreams. But a real dream from Heaven doesn't put you into a state of sedation where you just sit and mindlessly imagine how good life will be someday. When you have received a true word from God about His plan for your life, it should motivate you to *get busy* and make it happen! That dream should put a fire in your soul that's so hot, you simply *can't* sit around. It should turn you into a super-achiever who refuses to give up until your dream is fulfilled!

ELISHA'S CHARACTER BEFORE HIS DIVINE CALL

Elisha was a man who had built something successful with his life. He was a committed and faithful man. Because this type of success doesn't float to a person on clouds, we can be sure that Elisha worked very hard to achieve the success he had already experienced in life. No wonder God chose Elisha — he'd proven he could be trusted with an assignment!

The Bible is loaded with classic examples of what I'm telling you. The following list includes just a few examples of strategic, well-known, key Bible personalities who were *already* successful *before* God called them:

- *Noah* was successful and righteous *before* he was called to build the ark.

- *Abraham* was successful and rich *before* God called him to become the father of His covenant people.

- *Joshua* was successful as Moses' associate *before* God called him to be the leader of Israel.

- *David* was successful as a shepherd *before* God called him to be the next king of Israel.

- *Daniel* was successful in Nebuchadnezzar's court and walked in integrity *before* God's call came to him to be one of His prophets.

- *Matthew* was successful as a tax collector *before* Jesus called him to follow Him.

- *Peter* was a successful fisherman and businessman *before* Jesus called him to be His disciple.

- *Luke* was a successful doctor *before* he was called into the ministry.

- *Paul* was a successful politician and religious leader *before* God called him into the apostolic ministry.

- *Timothy* was successful as Paul's associate and disciple *before* he became the pastor of the church of Ephesus.

This is just a small, representative list of the many similar cases I could show you from both the Old and New Testaments. Let me encourage you to follow the example of these men of God by being faithful in what you put your hands to in this present season.

This also makes me think of Jesus' teaching in Matthew 25:29, where He said, "For unto every one that hath shall be given, and he shall have abundance: but from him that hath not shall be taken away even that which he hath."

In other words, how you perform in what you are doing *right now* may be the factor that determines whether or not God will call you to do something greater and more significant later. If you prove yourself faithful, God will know He can trust you with the next big promotion. Thus, the outcome of your future has a great deal to do with your present attitudes and job performance.

> How you perform in what you are doing *right now* may be the factor that determines whether or not God will call you to do something greater and more significant later.

It's important that you take a good look at yourself in order to honestly evaluate your current condition. So in light of what you've just read, ask yourself these questions:

- *How am I doing at my present job?*

- *Am I giving it 100 percent of my effort?*

- *If I were looking for someone to fill a position of great responsibility, would I want to hire someone who works like I do?*

- *Would I want to hire someone with an attitude like mine?*

- *Do I finish projects, or do I drop the ball along the way?*

- *Can I be trusted with money?*

- *Do I handle my money like I appreciate its value and power?*

- *Does my life and attitude reflect the qualities that would make God want to choose me?*

Your honest answers to these questions should help you determine whether or not you are the kind of person God wants to use. But don't despair if your answers were less than satisfactory. We're going to talk about how to make adjustments and become the kind of person God looks for when He needs someone to fulfill an assignment from Heaven!

TAKING STEPS
TO *GET* FREE AND *STAY* FREE

Although Denise and I are far from perfect, we've done our best to live our lives with the goal of staying *free* so we can do whatever God asks of us. We take deliberate care and attention to make sure nothing hinders us from obeying the Holy Spirit when He gives us a new assignment to fulfill. For instance, when we spend money, we ask ourselves: *Is this something that is going to affect our ability to obey the Lord? Can we do this and still be able to quickly act on what the Spirit of God tells us to do?*

From the very beginning of our marriage, Denise and I made it clear to our extended families that, although we love them, our highest aim in life is to follow God's call — even if it means we must live far away from them, at the farthest ends of the earth. By letting our family members know from the very beginning that we're serious about this commitment, they have never been too shocked when we've told them we are about to do something that will take us away from them.

Because we've always lived this kind of determined, purposeful life, our families *know* we will do whatever is needed to fulfill our life assignment. This knowledge makes it easier for them to accept our life of obedience, which then makes it easier for us as well.

You see, obeying God never means that we can ignore our family and abandon our finances for someone else to worry about. That would be very wrong! Finances are important and must be handled right. Family members are important and must be honored, respected, and loved. Responsibilities are also important and must not be shunned. Doing all things right as we step out to obey the Holy Spirit's leading is important to God.

Never forget that, as Jesus was dying on the Cross, He looked down and saw the young apostle John standing beside His own mother Mary. Then Jesus told John, "...Behold, thy mother!..." (John 19:27). At that moment, Jesus was bearing the weight of sin of all mankind in His tortured body. Nevertheless, instead of thinking about Himself, Jesus was thinking about who would care for His mother after He was gone.

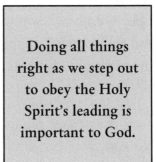

> Doing all things right as we step out to obey the Holy Spirit's leading is important to God.

The rest of the verse says, "...And from that hour that disciple took her unto his own home." But notice what the next verse states: "After this, Jesus knowing that all things were now accomplished..." (v. 28). In other words, one detail that Jesus considered essential was to make sure His mother would be taken of. Only then could He leave this earth knowing that everything had been accomplished.

Think of it — Jesus was departing the earth to become our Great High Priest. Yet making sure His mother's care was assured was important to Him. In speaking this word to John, Jesus was taking the final steps to becoming *unyoked* from the burden of this responsibility so He could fulfill His call.

Dream Thief Number Six:
Lack of Preparation

This leads us to another dream thief that has aborted many God-given dreams from ever being fulfilled: *the lack of necessary preparation* to pursue those dreams. Before we ever step out to obey God's call, we must make sure we've done everything we can to become equipped for the task and to get things in order in our lives — both naturally and spiritually.

In our years of living in the former Soviet Union, we have seen missionary families come and go, but not all of them left for good reasons. We've also observed that people tend to blame the devil for everything. Certainly, the devil does his fair share of bringing evil and problems into believers' lives. But everything bad that Christians experience cannot be blamed on the devil or on demonic attacks.

I can't count the times Denise and I have seen people quit their jobs and move their entire families to Russia, only to become so distracted by unresolved problems back home that they are never able to focus on their work in this mission field. There's no doubt these people were called. But because they left before taking care of their responsibilities, they couldn't focus on what God had called them to do. Too often we've seen missionaries pack up their families and go back home to deal with what they should have taken care of before they ever left in the first place. In some cases:

- They left before their house was sold or rented.

- They left before appointing someone to pay their bills.

- They left before raising sufficient financial support.

- They left before working out problems with relatives.

- They left before taking care of unresolved family issues.

One common scenario we've witnessed many times is a well-intentioned missionary family becoming financially strapped due to unresolved financial situations back home. Sadly, many of these families were finally forced to pack up and leave the place to which God had called them. Because they did things wrong before leaving on their faith journey, these people lost a lot of time and money and suffered a great deal of unnecessary emotional wear and tear. Only a few times have we seen any of these missionary families return. Most became so side tracked that they never made it back to the mission field where God called them.

> It may take a little longer to do things right the first time around. But nothing is as difficult as abandoning your call in order to go back and do what you should have done in the beginning.

It may take a little longer to do things right the first time around. But nothing is as difficult as abandoning your call in order to go back and do what you should have done in the beginning. Doing things right the first time is the smartest, cheapest, and best way to live!

Thanks to God and good counselors, our ministry has been able to stay where God has called us because we took the time to make sure all our responsibilities back home were covered. We have done whatever is necessary to have peace in our hearts that our family members are secure.

Denise and I and our ministry team have worked hard to communicate with our partner family, to keep our relationship with our partners alive, and to make them feel connected to what we are doing. As a result, we've been free to focus on the task before us without distractions that might pull us away from the call God has placed on our lives.

A great deal of effort has been required of us in order to remain in this position of freedom. It has often meant spending less money and moving a little slower on some projects. We might have wished those projects could have moved along a little faster. But in the long term, our efforts have empowered us to keep pressing forward into the apostolic territory where God has called this ministry. We know if we do things wrong, we'll only have to backtrack and fix the problem later. Therefore, rather than waste a lot of time and energy, we may as well do it right from the very start. In our own lives and ministry, we haven't always been successful at doing this, but this has been our goal.

It is wrong to run off to some other place and leave all your bills behind unpaid. It is wrong to yell good-bye to your family as you leave them without giving them some kind of explanation of what you are doing and reassuring them that you love them. It simply isn't right to ignore your responsibilities and leave others to deal with the problems you've abandoned in order to "follow God."

START TAKING ACTION *NOW!*

If you know God has called you, I urge you to start taking steps *now* to get free and to stay free so this scenario doesn't happen to you!

> It simply isn't right to ignore your responsibilities and leave others to deal with the problems you've abandoned in order to "follow God."

Even Elisha had a few things to take care of before he could follow Elijah. When Elijah called him, Elisha said, "...Let me, I pray thee, kiss my father and my mother, and then I will follow thee..." (1 Kings 19:20).

Elisha had real feelings for his family. He wanted to tell his family good-bye and make arrangements for his father and mother. These were some of the things he needed to do to get *unyoked* so he could follow God's plan for his life.

Elisha didn't want to leave any details back home undone or neglected. He wanted to move on to fulfill the call of God on his life with peace in his heart, knowing that he hadn't failed in his *natural* responsibilities. Elijah understood and appreciated Elisha's request. Therefore, the prophet told Elisha to go home and do what he needed to do.

When Jesus called His disciples into the ministry, they were *yoked* to some kind of job or responsibility. For instance, Matthew was *yoked* to the responsibilities of his job as a tax collector. Peter was *yoked* to the responsibility of running his fishing business. Similarly, we see that Elisha was *yoked* to his team of oxen and to his farming business when God's call came to him.

In order to do what God was asking of him, Elisha had to take steps to get free — to become *unyoked* — from his other responsibilities. He had to set his personal matters in order so he could follow God. *The steps Elisha took may be exactly what you need to do as well.*

Once You're Ready, Do Whatever You Must Do To Make Sure You Can Never Turn Back

Elisha went home to see his family before he left to follow Elijah. But while he was there, he did a most remarkable thing! The Bible says Elisha "...took a yoke of oxen, and slew them, and boiled their flesh with the instruments of the oxen, and gave unto the people, and they did eat..." (1 Kings 19:21).

I want you to understand exactly *what* Elisha did in front of his family that day and *why* he did it.

First, Elisha killed his oxen. Then he took the expensive wooden apparatus he used to drive the oxen and broke it into pieces. Finally, he used this wood to kindle a fire and cook his freshly killed oxen.

By doing this, Elisha was publicly burning every bridge behind him. He was sending a signal to his family, to his friends, and even to himself that this was *the point of no return*.

Likewise, when you know that God is asking *you* to step out of the status quo and move into His next season of purpose for your life, you'll need to do what Elisha did. Once you know you've taken care of all your responsibilities and have done all you need to do to prepare for your new assignment, it will be time to take the next step. Ask God what it means for you to reach that point of no return. What must you do to make sure you never turn back from following His will for your life?

> Ask God what it means for you to reach that point of no return. What must you do to make sure you never turn back from following His will for your life?

GOD CALLED SOMEONE WHO WAS WILLING TO BE RADICALLY OBEDIENT

The oxen Elisha killed were the engines of his farming business that drove his farming equipment. That machinery, now fueling the fire before him, was the equipment he used to break up the ground so he could plant the seeds that produced his annual harvest and income. That huge harvest each year gave Elisha financial security, which in turn gave him influence and position in his community.

Everything Elisha had achieved up to that point in his life — everything he had ever dreamed of becoming — was tied up in that team of oxen. Those oxen represented his *financial security* and *identity*.

What do you think Elisha felt as he watched the blood oozing from his oxen he'd just killed? What went through his mind as he heard the popping and crackling sounds of his wooden equipment burning in the blazing fire?

As Elisha stood there — looking at the fire that was burning his plowing equipment and cooking his dead oxen — he was saying farewell to his past. Everything in his present, as well as a major part of his plans for the future, was going up in smoke before his very eyes. There was no turning back now.

I'm sure the devil must have tormented Elisha's mind as he watched the farming equipment turn to ashes and the meat of the oxen cook in the fire that burned before him. As he took the cooked meat from the flames and put it on plates to serve to his family — and especially when he put the first bite of meat into his own mouth to eat — he must have wondered, *Dear God, what have I done?*

But this decision was permanent. There was no turning back. Elisha was ready to begin his God-ordained work, and he began it as a servant to the prophet Elijah. That's why verse 21 goes on to tell us, "...Then he arose, and went after Elijah, and ministered unto him."

Leaving the Past To Pursue His Future

Since there was nothing to hold him back now, Elisha turned his eyes toward the future. Rather than feel sorry for himself or allow the devil to torment him for what he had done, "...he arose, and went after Elijah, and ministered unto him."

By this time Elijah had moved on, so Elisha had to find him. Since Elijah was constantly on the move, it probably required some searching on Elisha's part to locate the prophet. But Elisha had determined that he would not stop until he found the man of God and took his place at Elijah's side. That's why the Bible says that Elisha *went after* Elijah.

In the same way, you can't wait for your divine call to chase you down. If you know that you're called and that it's time for you to step into your calling, you must choose to go after it and to pursue it with all your heart. Just "trying" to do the will of God will not work. You have to give 100 percent of yourself to the pursuit of God's call, or you surely will not succeed.

> Just "trying" to do the will of God will not work. You have to give 100 percent of yourself to the pursuit of God's call, or you surely will not succeed.

Elijah had a strong, forceful character. I'm sure he wasn't always the easiest person to serve. He may not have been the kind of person who said thank you very often. I just wonder if there were times that Elisha was sorry he had to work for Elijah.

Since Elisha was also a man of flesh, he probably had moments when he regretted killing his oxen, burning his equipment, and going to work for an "ingrate" like Elijah. Knowing the tendencies of pure flesh, I'm quite certain Elisha sometimes wished he could turn back the clock. But it was too late. He had invested too much to turn back.

It reminds me of the time people were leaving Jesus because of the difficult truths He was teaching them. But when Jesus turned to His disciples and asked, "Do you want to leave Me too?" they answered, "Where else would we go?" (*see* John 6:67,68). Jesus' disciples had walked with Him too long to turn back at that point, even though He gave them a window of opportunity to do so.

Don't Let the Yokes of This World Steal Your Dream

In Luke 14:16-24, Jesus told a parable about people who were called but who said, "I can't do it right now because I have other responsibilities!" Jesus was teaching that many people are called, but they often don't obey their divine mandate because they think they're too busy. These people are so yoked to the natural things of life that they just can't go with the flow and follow God. In the end, they give up, letting their excuses rob them of the dream He placed in their hearts.

In this passage of Scripture, Jesus said that people hesitate to follow Him for many reasons. He gave some of the excuses people use for not obeying His call:

- "I have property to manage."

- "I have oxen that I have to try out" (in other words, "I have business responsibilities I must attend to").

- "I have a wife and a family who need my attention."

I find it interesting that these are the same things that keep people from obeying God today. People allow themselves to be hindered from following God's call because of house payments, car payments, insurance payments, and work responsibilities or because of their spouse, children, grandparents, and other relatives. The list can go on and on.

Although we must be faithful and responsible in all these areas, we can't let any of them become a noose around our necks that paralyzes us and keeps us from pursuing the dream God has given us. That's why we must strive to stay free in our lives. When we answer His call, we must make the decision to give Him our all — to make a radical commitment of obedience from which we can never draw back again. We must decide to follow Jesus.

Of course, we can be sure that the devil will try to torment us from time to time. He will try to make us question where we are, what we've done, and the decisions we've made. But once we've made the choice to follow God's plan, we must set our faces like flint toward the future and focus totally on doing what He has called us to do. Any commitment less than this will result in our turning back, and, as God said in Hebrews 10:38, "...If any man draw back, my soul shall have no pleasure in him."

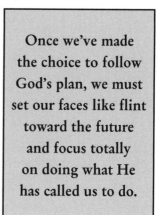

Once we've made the choice to follow God's plan, we must set our faces like flint toward the future and focus totally on doing what He has called us to do.

As Denise and I and our sons have obeyed God's will for our lives, we've concentrated on staying focused and not allowing the devil to torment us or make us question the road of obedience upon which we walk and live. There is no turning back for us. God has made His will clear to us, and we intend to follow it for the rest of our lives.

I want to encourage you to pursue the dream God has put in *your* heart. If you must take time to get unyoked from bills or responsibilities so you can obey, then begin the process today. Once you start on your road of obedience, make your obedience so radical that you can never turn back. Put your whole heart and soul into what God tells you to do. Elisha did, and, as a result, he received a double portion of Elijah's anointing!

The principle that worked for Elisha will work for you as well. God will honor and reward your actions of obedience as you get unhitched from the complexities of life to obey His call and pursue your dream!

THINK ABOUT IT

Does the phrase, "You can't get there from here" describe how you may feel at times when you think about God's calling on your life? What obstacles can you realistically identify that block your path? Write them down. They can be overcome, but you first need to develop a strategy to do so. Beside every obstacle you list, write down the solution to remove it.

The result is your plan of action — what you need to do or what you need to believe in faith for *God* to do. When you do your part, God has guaranteed to do His part to help you. His Son's own blood is already on the line to assure your victory.

God gives to those who actively use what they have. He knows that the faithful and productive person will continue to be faithful and productive and that laziness is the fast track to a fruitless life.

God will not give you more if you are sloppy or squandering what you already possess. So honestly examine your lifestyle choices and your attitudes. Are you lazy in any area or responsibility? This is the time to change. If you have a God-given dream that is ever to be more than a fantasy, its manifestation will require your hard work, your aggressive faith, and your steadfast determination to fulfill every responsibility. What are you waiting on?

Focus on the day-by-day work of building solid habits of responsibility in preparation for your dream to come to pass. If the opportunity of a lifetime showed up for you today, would you be prepared to take it?

Now is the time to cultivate the character that will equip you to fulfill your calling. Weak character can sabotage a great dream.

Are you allowing any habits, pastimes, associations, or attitudes to slow down your preparation and progress? Your divinely ordained moment will come. Your gifts may escort you through a door, but will your character allow you to remain in the room your dream has destined you to occupy?

CHAPTER EIGHT

A THREEFOLD CORD
IS NOT QUICKLY BROKEN

*M*y deep desire is that this book will provoke you to seek God fervently for your life's plan and purpose, if He hasn't already spoken to you. I also pray that once you know what He has called you to do, you will be equally provoked to follow the Holy Spirit's leading and take the necessary steps to bring that divine plan to pass in your life. However, in provoking you "unto love and to good works" (Hebrews 10:24), I would be grossly negligent if I didn't remind you of one extremely important fact: *You are not alone in this great adventure!*

First and foremost, you have Jesus' promise that He will never leave you or forsake you (Hebrews 13:5). This, of course, is the most important and preeminent truth you must never lose sight of. Jesus should always be your ultimate focus as you begin to pursue His purposes for your life.

But I also want to stress that when you begin to take steps to make your dream a reality, God will place other people in your life to assist you. He brings these relationships into your life for the purpose of encouraging and provoking you to respond correctly as difficult situations arise. And I guarantee you that difficult situations *will* arise as the enemy tries to stop God's plan from being fulfilled in your life!

There are two fundamental reasons why we succumb to the tactics of the dream thieves and forsake our vision. The first involves our individual walk with the Lord. We must guard our hearts and minds by spending time in His Word and praying for divine guidance and strength from the Holy Spirit. Essentially, every chapter in this book until now has dealt with different aspects of maintaining a strong, enduring relationship with God.

But the second reason we lose our passion and abandon our dream concerns our relationships within the Body of Christ.

> **God never intended for us to live out our lives of faith alone.**

Sometimes after much time has passed since we received our word from God, we carry an enormous burden of discouragement yet fail to turn to other believers for help and support. However, God never intended for us to live out our lives of faith alone.

DREAM THIEF NUMBER SEVEN:
ISOLATION

In the book of Ecclesiastes, Solomon wrote several verses of Scripture that indicate he understood that "no man is an island unto himself." The message in these verses is clear: *We need each other as we endeavor to carry out the dreams God gives us.*

Two are better than one; because they have a good reward for their labour. For if they fall, the one will lift up his fellow: but woe to him that is alone when he falleth; for he hath not another to help him up. Again, if two lie together, then they have heat: but how can one be warm alone? And if one prevail against him, two shall withstand him; and a threefold cord is not quickly broken.

Ecclesiastes 4:9-12

We've already talked about the dream thieves of *time, Satan, friends, family, neutrality,* and *lack of preparation.* Another dream thief we must contend with as believers is *isolation.* If the enemy can succeed in isolating us from our brothers and sisters in Christ, he can stop our spiritual growth in its tracks and make it nearly impossible for us to fulfill our divine destiny.

Now, I'm not referring to those believers who suffer in isolation in political prisons or in similar situations, separated from other believers against their will. Certainly, the Bible tells us that God gives special grace and comfort to these precious brothers and sisters. I'm also not referring to believers who schedule times of *solitude* to seek God or to get some needed rest and refreshing.

I am talking about Christians who, in the normal course of life, swallow lie after lie from the enemy — lies such as:

- *No one really likes me.*

- *No one has ever had the problem or weakness I struggle with.*

- *No one would like me if I ever opened up and shared who I really am.*

- *What do I have to offer anyone anyway?*

Finally, these people retreat within themselves, hiding themselves away until they have become isolated and alone.

Another unfortunate scenario occurs when believers are offended or hurt by other believers and use their offenses or broken hearts as an excuse to withdraw from *all* believers. These people decide in their minds that all Christians are exactly like the one who hurt or offended them. In their anger and unforgiveness, they turn from the Church and pursue friendships in the world instead.

Perhaps you've also been tempted to isolate yourself from other believers after receiving a word from God. Maybe you encountered rejection from family or friends. You may feel like drawing away from everyone and everything involved in the local church because of some hurt or disappointment. Or your mind may have been bombarded with lies from the enemy as you kept trying to remain steadfast through the passing of time.

> To allow yourself to become isolated and separated from the rest of the Body of Christ or from spiritual authority under *any* circumstances can be deadly to your walk with God and to the ultimate fulfillment of your dream.

However, be forewarned: To allow yourself to become isolated and separated from the rest of the Body of Christ or from spiritual authority under ANY circumstances can be deadly to your walk with God and to the ultimate fulfillment of your dream.

Isolating yourself is never the solution. And it's important to realize that isolation isn't just a matter of physically distancing yourself from fellowship with other believers, from your local church, or from spiritual authority. You can also disengage and detach yourself emotionally and spiritually so that, even though you sit in the midst of the congregation each week, you still miss out on the supply of strength and encouragement your fellow believers could provide you.

Of course, when you feel like isolating yourself from other believers, your first step should be to draw near to God. He will provide the strength and healing you need from any hurt or disappointment you may have experienced. Then you'll find that not only will He heal your pain, but He will also direct people into your life to express His love toward you and knit you into the family of God in a healthy way.

Isolation does *not* heal pain; in fact, it actually creates more problems by making you an open target for the enemy's devices. God designed godly fellowship to be a protective measure in your life. That's what Ecclesiastes 4:9,10 means when it states, "Two are better than one... For if they fall, the one will lift up his fellow: but woe to him that is alone when he falleth; for he hath not another to help him up."

You see, it's true that through faith and patience, we inherit the promises of God. However, our faith and our ability to endure can suffer tremendously if we live isolated and alone, disconnected from the Church. We need the love and encouragement of other believers — not only to help us fulfill our dreams, but also to help us grow up spiritually, keep our lives in check, and remain stable in our walk with God.

So don't entertain thoughts of pulling away from people, particularly when you're hurting or when you're tempted to let go of your dream. The enemy will try to inject those negative thoughts into your mind like a hook to pull you into isolation so he can intensify his attack against you. Whenever you start thinking like that, you must recognize that, now more than ever, you need those close brothers and sisters God has brought into your life!

Remember, even Jesus needed the fellowship of His closest friends during a time of great inner anguish. That's the reason He asked Peter, James, and John to pray with Him in the Garden of Gethsemane on the night before His crucifixion.

Too many people never take their place in the Body of Christ because they fail to enter into daily fellowship with other believers or to make the effort to integrate other brothers and sisters in Christ into their lives. They are afraid to confess their weaknesses to a friend, to admit they need some help, or even to ask for prayer. If these believers continue giving in to the enemy's isolationist tactics, it won't be long before their ability to endure the great fight of afflictions will become more and more diminished. Then one day when they suffer one of life's devastating blows that they can't endure alone, they will be much more likely to give up or to become neutral in their walk with God.

Faith comes from God and is nurtured by His Word as we have communion with and receive guidance from the Holy

Spirit. However, God intends for us to receive a great deal of the Word from other believers as well. That's why He commands us to "...exhort one another daily, while it is called To day; lest any of you be hardened through the deceitfulness of sin" (Hebrews 3:13). In addition, the Bible tells us that "...faith without works is dead..." (James 2:26). As we rub shoulders with other saints in the local church, we have ample opportunity to put the Word to work in our lives!

Patience also comes from God, and it is developed as we choose to continue loving and serving Him with all our hearts, souls, minds, and strength — no matter what obstacles are thrown in our path. But again, our patience is strengthened as other believers come alongside us and share the victories and joys they have fought hard to attain themselves.

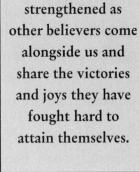

Our patience is strengthened as other believers come alongside us and share the victories and joys they have fought hard to attain themselves.

This is why the Holy Spirit will often send another believer to fortify you and help you renew your passion and zeal when you're out of touch in your walk with God. That friend in Christ will help reconnect you with the power of God's Word and the fire of the Holy Spirit. And if you're holding fast to your faith and patience, your godly friend will help stir up the fire already burning in your heart, inspiring you to boldly fulfill your divine destiny.

This is the "threefold cord" Solomon was referring to: *you, your godly friend*, and *God*. Jesus tells us in Matthew 18:19,20 that whenever you and another believer agree in prayer, He is present —

ready to release His awesome, supernatural power and perform His Word on your behalf. *Therefore, the threefold cord is a key to fulfilling your divine destiny!*

Faith and patience reach maturity in your life as you get involved in your church, fellowshipping and making close friendships with other believers in that local body. On the other hand, without daily contact with the people God has ordained for you to be in close relationship with, you can be deceived into thinking that you're growing and maturing in the Lord when, in reality, you're not.

Absolutely no faith or patience is required to sit at home and watch Christian television. As you sit in your comfortable easy chair or recline on your sofa watching television, you are in total control of the situation. You can choose what suits you at any given time, and no one is challenging you on any level of your life.

Even if you're deeply moved by a television minister's dynamic teaching from the Word, no one is there to hold you accountable for living out that teaching. You may never feel compelled to apply the teachings you hear to your daily life because you're not associating with fellow Christians or placing yourself in any situations that require you to act on what you've learned. Of course, the Holy Spirit is always present, and He will prod you and convict you to a certain degree. However, it's a lot easier to ignore the Holy Spirit when no one else is around to remind you of what He's saying!

Bearing One Another's Burdens

At this point, you may be asking, "Well, just how involved in other people's lives do I have to get? How much of their lives is my responsibility, and how much is their own responsibility?"

In this day and age when "co-dependency" is so prevalent, even believers can develop an abnormal dependency on another person, making an individual the source of their strength and life instead of the Lord Jesus Christ. We in the Church must find the scriptural balance for godly relationships.

The Bible gives us insight along this line in Galatians 6:2-5:

> **Bear ye one another's burdens, and so fulfil the law of Christ. For if a man think himself to be something, when he is nothing, he deceiveth himself. But let every man prove his own work, and then shall he have rejoicing in himself alone, and not in another. For every man shall bear his own burden.**

At first glance, it appears that these verses of Scripture contain a contradiction. Paul states in verse 2, "Bear ye one another's burdens...." But then in verse 5, he says, "For every man shall bear his own burden." What is the Holy Spirit trying to tell us in these verses?

First, the Greek word for "burden" in verse 2 is *baros*, which refers to *a heavy or crushing weight, whether physical or spiritual, that presses against a person, making him feel burdened or weighed down.* In other words, this isn't a normal, everyday type of burden;

rather, it's a burden beyond what people experience in the normal course of life.

This type of pressing burden might be a habitual sin that has plagued you and weighed you down year after year of your life. If that's the case, Satan will try to use that weakness or fault to hinder or completely abort the plan of God for your life. That's why any lingering *baros* burdens of sin in your life must be dealt with and defeated. If you're unable to do it alone, you need to seek the help of others to pull you through to a place of victory.

This is such an important point to understand. We all have areas in our lives that are filthy and totally repugnant to God — if not always to ourselves. We've all sinned and fallen short of His glory (Romans 3:23). However, we must not allow these areas to run and ultimately ruin our lives. Instead, we should look these strongholds boldly in the face and deal with them straightforwardly. And in the process, we should never allow fear or pride to intimidate us from getting the help we need from our brothers and sisters in Christ.

> We should never allow fear or pride to intimidate us from getting the help we need from our brothers and sisters in Christ.

The writer of Hebrews strongly exhorts us in Hebrews 12:1 to "...lay aside every weight, and the sin which doth so easily beset us, and let us run with patience the race that is set before us." Let me stress again: When a sin is a heavy weight that is constantly pressing against our lives, causing us to become twisted and bent out of shape in our souls, we will need the love and assistance of other believers to overcome that sinful stronghold once and for all. In that kind of situation, the Lord will give us godly friends who will pray for us, counsel us with His Word, and help us experience victory. Most importantly, it is often the unconditional love, compassion, and understanding of our close brothers and sisters in Christ — those who cherish us for who we really are in the Lord and look beyond our present struggle to see us standing in truth — that bring us to our knees in worship to the One who inspired their love.

A besetting sin in our lives isn't the only weight that can press against us. A pressing burden can also be something good and godly, such as a vision or dream God gives us in order to see His plans and purposes carried out on the earth. When we're carrying this kind of burden, our natural minds can't fathom how He will bring to pass what He has spoken to us, and we realize that we cannot carry out our divine assignment by ourselves.

God will bring us "support from Zion" when we are faced with this type of burden (Psalm 20:1 *NIV*). He may have given us something to do that goes beyond our natural abilities and gifts to accomplish. But when the weight of our divine assignment is pressing in on us, God will bring brothers and sisters into our lives who not only will encourage and refresh us spiritually, but will also help us carry out the vision in natural, practical ways.

For example, I think of that day years ago when the Holy Spirit spoke to my heart about moving my family to the Soviet Union to teach in a Bible school and to help establish other churches throughout that region of the world. When I

> When the weight of our divine assignment is pressing in on us, God will bring brothers and sisters into our lives who not only will encourage and refresh us spiritually, but will also help us carry out the vision in natural, practical ways.

understood what the Lord was asking me to do, I immediately recognized that this was a burden I would require some help in carrying! This vision was like a weight pressing against my heart and mind, so I began to look for other believers who would help me obey the word I'd received from the Lord and ease the weight of my burden.

Some of the friends God sent me have been for encouragement and counsel; others have been sent to supply needs and to help me carry out this awesome task. Regardless of their various roles in my life, I am forever grateful to God that He led these individuals to help me, minister to me, and be my friends.

In addition, God has put in my life a small group of committed Christian leaders to whom I am accountable in every area of life and ministry. Denise and I both realize that these particular relationships have been crucial to our lives and have demonstrated to us again and again the safety found in maintaining accountability. These spiritual leaders, who have also been the truest of friends, have walked with me through some of the darkest valleys of my life. I can truthfully say that their steadfast love and care for my soul is one reason Denise and I have been able to overcome the huge challenges we've faced in our lives and ministry. They have lovingly listened to me, inspired me, confronted me — and, at times, they have rebuked me and required repentance when I've erred. I'm thankful that God put these men in my life, and I know they'll reap an eternal reward for always being there for me and for so willingly helping Denise and me impact thousands of lives.

Let's move on to look at Galatians 6:5, which states, "For every man shall bear his own burden." Here the word "burden" is the Greek word *phortion*, which refers to *the normal load that every person must carry*. This verse reminds us that there is a certain amount of responsibility *we* are required to carry *ourselves*. No one can do our work for us, and no one can make our decisions for us. This is the "proving" referred to in verse 4: We must prove our faith and develop our patience to inherit the Lord's promises — and that means acting on His Word and living it *ourselves*.

This type of burden will not wear us out or weigh us down. It involves the everyday business of living the Christian life and doing what God has called us to do day after day. Jesus used the same word when He said, "...My yoke is easy, and my *burden* is light" (Matthew 11:30).

Many of the things we've discussed in this book are examples of the burdens we're to deal with on our own by the Word and the Holy Spirit.

- We must choose to believe God's Word and hold fast to what He has spoken to us.

- We must imitate those who demonstrate great faith and perseverance.

- We must not allow ourselves to become neutral in our walk with God.

- We must develop both faith and patience and learn to endure with rejoicing.

These are all elements of the normal burden each of us must personally bear. No one can do these things for us.

However, eventually God may ask you to accomplish something monumental in your lifetime — a task or series of tasks that go far beyond your own capabilities and gifts alone. Or perhaps the Lord will require you to put away a sin that has held you in its grip for years and that you've been unable to overcome by your own efforts. At these times, you will discover that you need the help of other believers in order to fulfill your divine destiny. In the same way, it will be your role at times to help others press on and overcome so *their* God-given dreams can come to pass.

Again, your friends in the Lord — those who have been divinely connected to you — will not only join you under the burden that is beyond your ability to fulfill or conquer by yourself, but they will ultimately cause you to become dependent on Jesus, not on them, as they impel you to look to Him as your first love. They will get you back on track with the Holy Spirit and help fill you with the Word of God. After you have talked with them or spent time with them, you will walk away with a renewed passion for the things of God and a solid confidence that "...he which hath begun a good work in you will perform it until the day of Jesus Christ" (Philippians 1:6).

Thus, one of the most astounding results of carrying out God's will for your life is this: *The dreams God gives you will bring with them some of the most ful filling and satisfying relationships of your life.*

Consider One Another

Through passages of Scripture such as the one we just discussed in Galatians 6, we are adding another dimension of truth, another piece of the puzzle, that will help us carry out the vision God has given us. Simply stated, the principle is this: God has provided the local church to the Body of Christ as the answer for the dream thief of isolation. This principle is also found in Hebrews 10:24,25:

> The dreams God gives you will bring with them some of the most fulfilling and satisfying relationships of your life.

> **And let us consider one another to provoke unto love and to good works: not forsaking the assembling of ourselves together, as the manner of some is; but exhorting one another: and so much the more, as ye see the day approaching.**

The word "consider" in verse 24 is the Greek word *katanoeo*. The word *kata* depicts *something that is moving downward*, and *noeo* refers to *the mind* or *the thinking process*. When the two words are compounded together, the new word means *to consider something thoroughly, all the way through, from top to bottom, from A to Z.*

The local church was meant to be a place where believers would come to corporately worship the Lord, to hear His Word, and to "consider one another." The idea behind "consider one another" is that we observe and contemplate each other so intently and so thoroughly that we begin to perceive each other's situations as they really are. In other words, *we help each other have a realistic view of our lives.*

We might paraphrase this verse this way: *"And observe one another; contemplate one another; have a realistic view of one another; take mental notes when you see certain characteristics in one another, and mark them down in your mind."* This is a description of mutual encouragement in the local church. We are to be very concerned about one another's well-being.

For example, you may take note of a person in the church who is discouraged and then find out it doesn't take too much effort to encourage him. With just a word here and a word there, you're able to put that fellow believer in remembrance of God's faithfulness and His provision for him.

Subsequently, you may witness someone else in the church who is believing God for something and has yet to see any results. Maybe it takes a little more effort to encourage this believer. You find that he needs you to not only give him the Word, but also to *demonstrate* the Word by spending time with him and showing him that he's special to you and to God. You then make a mental note of what was required to help him so you know how to assist him again in the future.

Why is this process important? Because God wants us to get involved in the local church, not just to receive for ourselves but also to help others receive from the Lord. We all need loving relationships within the Body of Christ — people who will love us, observe us, and support us when we're standing on a word from God and doing all we know to do to bring that vision into reality.

However, as I've pointed out before, it's often necessary for a believer to ask for someone's help in order to receive the supply of strength or wisdom he or she needs. Too many times Christians have a difficult time asking someone else to pray with them, listen to their problems, or provide good, godly counsel. But the root of someone's unwillingness to open up and ask other believers for help is usually *pride*, a sin that all believers must diligently guard against in their lives.

> We all need loving relationships within the Body of Christ — people who will love us, observe us, and support us when we're standing on a word from God and doing all we know to do to bring that vision into reality.

Proverbs 17:17 states, "A friend loveth at all times, and a brother is born for adversity." This verse is saying that your real friends will love you no matter what you're going through. God intends for you to develop these types of close friendships with other brothers and sisters in Christ. These special people He brings into your life will be there to assist you whenever you experience difficult and challenging times.

I'm not implying that we should sit around, nurturing our sorrows and dwelling on our difficulties. But there are times the Lord will lead us to share our troubles with a godly confidant for the sake of receiving needed encouragement or obtaining wisdom on how to deal with a situation. We should *not* share our problems with another believer just so we can rehearse defeat after defeat in our lives and continue feeling sorry for ourselves.

Likewise, God designed the local church to be a place of victory where faith is built up, the soul is encouraged, and wisdom and strength are imparted. It's to be a community where faith lives and triumphs through love and concern for one another. There is nothing like living in an atmosphere of faith and love where you're surrounded by believers who really believe the Word of God and practice it. No matter what challenge you're facing, you can receive from God in a place like this.

And this blessing of fellowship extends both ways, for there is absolutely no substitute for the joy and satisfaction that comes when you help a brother or sister in your church rise up out of the depths of despair to the heights of hope and faith again. Although a person may be desperately striving to "hold fast" and may feel like his grip on his divine destiny is slipping, you will be able to assist him because you have "considered" him, observed him, and made mental notes about him as the Bible commands.

BE A 'HOLY PROVOKER'

Not only are we exhorted to "consider one another," but Hebrews 10:24 goes on to say we are to "...*provoke* unto love and to good works...." The Greek word translated "provoke" is *paraxusmos*, a compound word made up of the words *para* and *xusmos*. The word *para* means *to be as close as you can possibly get,* and *xusmos* means *to sharpen*, as in sharpening a knife or indicating a very sharp situation.

When you put the two words together, the new word describes *someone who has attached himself to another person's life and is intent on continuously prodding and impelling that person to a certain action* — in this case, "unto love and to good works."

You may have already guessed that "provoking" one another can be either a positive or a negative action! One meaning of this word could be *to call into combat*. Throughout the New Testament, the word *paraxusmos* is usually translated to mean *to irritate, to incite to anger, to inflame, or to enrage*. Obviously, all of these meanings refer to provoking someone in order to bring forth a negative result.

However, in Hebrews 10:24, the Word of God is actually telling us that our relationships should evoke a response of godliness and faith. We should continually be sharpening one another — inciting one another to become better, stronger, and bolder in the Lord.

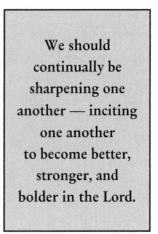

We should continually be sharpening one another — inciting one another to become better, stronger, and bolder in the Lord.

How can we provoke one another in a positive way? What does it mean to stimulate our brothers and sisters in such a way that we make them want to walk in love and do good works? How can we sharpen a fellow believer who wants to walk in faith or inspire another person in need of endurance?

One day my wife Denise provided me with a perfect example that helps answer these questions.

I had just preached a message on how the Body of Christ should encourage one another. As Denise and I walked out of the auditorium, I could tell she was very excited about it. I, however, had come under intense condemnation from the enemy and was convinced that my message was absolutely the worst I had ever preached.

Sensing my wife's enthusiasm, I blurted out before she could say anything to me, "That was the worst sermon I've ever preached in my life!" At that moment, I firmly believed those words. I considered my message a complete and total failure, and I didn't want her telling me anything to the contrary.

Nevertheless, Denise responded, "Oh, Honey, it was a wonderful message!" In my state of mind, I was convinced that my wife was saying these things only because my sermon had addressed how Christians should encourage one another and that she was now sacrificing the truth in order to apply my message to the situation!

I turned to Denise and said, "Don't lie to me in the name of encouragement! The message was horrible, and I *know* it was horrible!"

Undaunted, Denise answered, "But it *wasn't* horrible! My heart was deeply touched. I'm changed because of what you preached today."

"That's the last time I'm preaching that message," I said angrily. "If you're going to walk out of that service telling me that my message was good in the name of encouragement, I'm not going to let you encourage me anymore! I know for a fact that it was a flop! I want you to be honest and tell me how miserable the message was today!"

As for Denise on the day we had that conversation, she was so persistent that I finally told her to be quiet; I didn't want to hear anything she had to say. Nevertheless, she just kept right on prodding and hounding me with uplifting remarks and loving words of encouragement. She said, "Honey, I am *not* going to be quiet, because the Word says I should encourage you."

Denise continued to provoke me all the way from anger and despair right back to the middle of God's will. After a while, I gave in to her encouragement. My wife had come alongside me, attached herself closely to me, and loved me so much that she refused to leave me in self-defeat. She sharpened me. She prodded me. She impelled and inspired me.

Every believer needs to be lovingly provoked at times, irrespective of his or her position in the Body of Christ — and the greatest men and women of God are no exception. Even the most anointed servants of the Lord are still subject to the wiles of the devil and the lies of the flesh, just like anyone else. Everyone needs a loving push in the right direction now and then!

Of course, there will be times when the Holy Spirit uses a brother or sister in Christ to lovingly but firmly point out serious errors in judgment or sin in a fellow believer's life. Paul speaks of this in Galatians 6:1: "Brethren, if a man be overtaken in a fault, ye which are spiritual, restore such an one in the spirit of meekness; considering thyself, lest thou also be tempted."

Let's consider again the incident I just related when Denise provoked me until I broke free of the devil's lies. My dear wife would have responded differently if I'd said something during my message that was either personally offensive to someone or scripturally unsound. I'm certain she would have prayerfully and lovingly brought that fact to my attention!

At times God will call upon us to set someone else straight on an issue or urge another believer to deal honestly and straightforwardly with sin in his or her life. In those situations, we need to remember that we're also called to provoke and inspire that person unto love and good works, not unto condemnation and self-loathing. In all such situations, our motivation should be to see our fellow believers set free from every hindrance or weight that would prohibit them from being all they are called to be in Christ.

> In all situations, our motivation should be to see our fellow believers set free from every hindrance or weight that would prohibit them from being all they are called to be in Christ.

We all know how to provoke each other in the negative sense, so why don't we commit ourselves to becoming equally proficient in provoking one another in ways that are positive and life-giving? The Bible tells us how to do it: We are to consider, observe, contemplate, and think all the way through the matter of *becoming experts at provoking one another unto love and good deeds*!

Sanctified Addiction

Another verse of Scripture I want you to consider is Acts 2:42, which reads, "And they *continued stedfastly* in the apostles' doctrine and fellowship, and in breaking of bread, and in prayers." Notice the phrase, "continued steadfastly." This is a very interesting phrase. You could say it carries the notion of an *addiction*. In other words, receiving the teaching of the Word and enjoying fellowship with other believers became so important to these early believers that they couldn't live without these aspects of their walk with God.

Consider for a moment the characteristics of an *unhealthy* addiction. For instance, we know that a heroin addict can't make it through a day without heroin. Without taking the drug on a daily basis, the addict will go through incredible withdrawal pain and mental trauma.

An addict's craving provides a vivid analogy of the positive addiction that developed among the saints in Acts 2:42. They couldn't go through one day without spending times of fellowship together to discuss the Word of God.

The truth is, God has created each individual member of the Body of Christ to function interdependently. Each of us is designed to require a supply from other brothers and sisters in Christ, as well as to release a supply of strength toward our fellow believers. This kind of close fellowship is crucial for both our spiritual and emotional well-being. Without the opportunity to receive or to release that supply of encouragement and support, we become spiritually deficient and susceptible to becoming traumatized by the enemy's deception. In this sense, God intends for us to be *addicted* to close fellowship with godly believers.

The fellowship among the early believers was so encouraging and produced such a close community of faith that "...fear came upon every soul: and many wonders and signs were done by the apostles" (Acts 2:43). These men and women were totally committed to their Lord and to each other. They lifted up one another when the dreams God had placed in their hearts began to fade in the face of adversity and persecution. And the Bible says that as a result of their faithfulness and loyalty to one another, the Lord performed many supernatural signs and wonders in their midst.

There is another significant purpose for having a healthy addiction to — or a passionate devotion for — godly fellowship with one another daily. Hebrews 3:12,13 says, "Take heed, brethren, lest there be in any of you an evil heart of unbelief, in departing from the living God. *But exhort one another daily....*"

Whenever the Bible talks about departing from the living God, it isn't referring to something you do in one day. You don't just wake up one morning and suddenly decide to backslide or to stop fellowshipping with your Heavenly Father. This word "departing" is the Greek word *aphistimi*, which carries the idea of *removing oneself* or *taking a step away from*. This latter meaning implies a gradual movement away from something. You take a step away from the dream God gave you — and then another step and another. In a sense, you are slowly changing your position. Initially you are still standing on your word from the Lord, but your stance is progressively becoming more distant from the promises God planted in your heart.

This verse is saying that we depart from the living God through an "evil heart of unbelief." What causes this terrible state of mind and heart? Verse 13 tells us: *Disobedience to the divine command to "…exhort one another daily…."* Believers are to fellowship with other brothers and sisters in Christ on a daily basis so all can mutually exhort one another to hold fast to God's Word. In other words, a person's failure to pursue daily fellowship with other godly believers centered around the Word of God can eventually cause that person to develop an evil heart of unbelief.

> A person's failure to pursue daily fellowship with other godly believers centered around the Word of God can eventually cause that person to develop an evil heart of unbelief.

When you're not sharing your life with other believers and you're carrying all your burdens on your own, you get tired and worn out. You need the passion of other believers whom God will bring into your life to keep your own dreams fresh and alive. As Hebrews 3:12,13 warns, when you stop fellowshipping with others of like faith, it won't be long before you break fellowship with the Lord.

In verse 13, the Greek word for "exhort" is *parakaleo*, which is a compound of *para*, meaning *alongside*, and *kaleo*, meaning *to call out to someone* or *to invite someone*. *Parakaleo* is the very same word Jesus used in John 14:16 to describe the Holy Spirit as the Comforter. When you exhort another believer, in a very real sense you are participating in the ministry of the Holy Spirit.

Also, the word *para* returns to the concepts of provoking one another unto love and good works and having a healthy, godly addiction to one another. We are to attach ourselves to the believers with whom God has called us to be strongly connected, allowing Him to draw us as close to them as He desires. He wants us to lovingly get involved in each other's lives, looking for opportunities to encourage and support one another in whatever way we can. We are to be "addicted" to one another, recognizing that we cannot be successful in our walk with God without the mutual encouragement we find in each other's fellowship.

This verse in Hebrews also says that you need this kind of fellowship *every day*. If you live alone, make sure you have some form of contact with other believers on a daily basis. Fellowship in the Body of Christ must extend beyond the church walls and into your everyday life. Verses 13 and 14 go on to explain why this is so important:

> But exhort one another daily, while it is called To day; lest any of you be hardened through the deceitfulness of sin. For we are made partakers of Christ, if we hold the beginning of our confidence stedfast unto the end.

> Hebrews 3:13,14

According to verse 13, if we forsake daily fellowship and mutual encouragement with other believers, sin can easily deceive us and harden our hearts tothe things of God. Then verse 14 goes on to say that we also risk losing our inheritance if we don't "hold fast" our confidence to the end — and part of our inheritance is God's divine destiny for our lives.

The Bible clearly teaches us that *in Christ* we are partakers of everything Jesus purchased for us — salvation, authority over the devil, prosperity, health, deliverance, and a life full of meaning and purpose. But the Word of God qualifies this truth by letting us know that the only way we will actually enter into union with these promises is to "...hold the beginning of our confidence stedfast unto the end."

> If we forsake daily fellowship and mutual encouragement with other believers, sin can easily deceive us and harden our hearts to the things of God.

These verses of Scripture make it abundantly clear that one of the keys for "holding fast" is to remain in close fellowship with other believers, both receiving and giving daily encouragement and support. The next five verses go on to provide a biblical illustration of what the Holy Spirit is telling us along this line:

> While it is said, To day if ye will hear his voice, harden not your hearts, as in the provocation. For some, when they had heard, did provoke: howbeit not all that came out of Egypt by Moses. But with whom was he grieved forty years? was it not with them that had sinned, whose carcases fell in the wilderness? And to whom sware he that they should not enter into his rest, but to them that believed not?

> So we see that they could not enter in because of unbelief.
>
> ### Hebrews 3:15-19

Notice that the writer of Hebrews uses the word "provoke" in verse 16 in the negative context. When the 12 spies returned from the Promised Land to make their report to Moses, only two of them gave an encouraging, faith-filled report, declaring, "We are well able to take the land!" (*see* Numbers 13:30). The other ten gave a negative report.

Rather than believing the victory report, most of the Israelites agreed with the ten doubting spies and began provoking one another in a negative way. They probably made comments such as, "What do you mean, 'We are well able'? Quit lying to us in the name of God, and start being realistic. If there are giants living in Canaan, we certainly can't take the land!"

And this passage of Scripture tells it all: The people hardened their hearts and grieved the Lord, a choice that resulted in their wandering in the wilderness for 40 years and ultimately dying there. Because they "believed not," they never entered the Promised Land or saw the fulfillment of their dream. The Greek literally says, "They refused to be persuaded." The multitude who turned a deaf ear to the word of faith and victory — who rebelled against the two spies who were provoking them to fulfill the will of God — died in the desert long after the passion for their dream of the Promised Land had been quenched by unbelief.

If you are believing God for the fulfillment of a dream He has planted in your heart, you can rest assured that you *will* encounter giants as you seek to enter your promised land. As you face these challenges to your faith, this is *not* the time to hang around believers who habitually and stubbornly walk according to their own understanding. Those who are ruled by their own emotions and not by God's Word are often filled with bitterness and disappointment. If you attach yourself closely to people like that, they may very well provoke you unto doubt, unbelief, and a hardened heart.

In order to fulfill God's plan for your life, ask Him to connect you with faith-filled, uplifting believers. You need brothers and sisters who will lovingly attach themselves to you, making observations and watching your life in order to provoke you unto love and good deeds — and they need you to do the same for them. That's what the local church is all about!

Certainly there will be specific times when God calls us to stand alone, as Daniel did in the lions' den, or draws us aside for a special time alone with Him. But for the most part, we are called to connect with the Body of Christ on a daily basis — to stand with one another, bear one another's burdens, consider one another, provoke one another unto good works, and be addicted to each other.

Consider Shadrach, Meshach, and Abednego — who took strength from each other as they refused to bow before an idol of the king (*see* Daniel chapter 3). Consider the early believers in Acts 2:42, who were "addicted" to each other and to the Word. Like these godly men and women, we will not only see our vision become reality, but we will also experience more deeply the ways and presence of the Lord through the joy of knowing and loving one another.

THINK ABOUT IT

Your visions and dreams can bring you into connection with some of the most fulfilling and satisfying relationships in your life. Can you identify the people God has positioned in your life to strengthen you and to provoke you unto love and good works?

Encouragement is one of the most profound gifts you can bring to the life of another person. Your words can lift someone from the depths of despair to the heights of hope.

Do you endeavor to take notice of those around you — to recognize when someone may need the strength of your encouragement? Stay alert, and watch for people in your life who may be desperately striving to "hold fast" to their faith while feeling as though their grip is slipping. Each day make a conscious effort to yield to the Holy Spirit so the God of all comfort can speak through you to make a difference in someone's life.

Friendships centered on the truth of God's Word can shield you from faltering in your fellowship with the Lord. Conversely, friendships rooted in carnal pursuits or supported with worldly attitudes can serve as the fast track to failure in life.

Who are the dominant influences in your life, and how are they influencing you — for better or for worse?

Are you drawn to an association that has caused the vision of your purpose in life to grow dim? If so, you are in danger of derailing your dream by becoming attached to a dream thief. Associations for God and for good will inspire you to see and to become *more*, not *less*.

Evaluate the quality of your associations and activities in light of your God-given dream; then, if necessary, make adjustments as the Holy Spirit leads.

Has jealousy, negativity, or fear caused you to become a dream thief in someone else's life?

CHAPTER NINE

THE POWER OF YOUR WILL

*W*e all have crossroads in our lives — moments in time in which God speaks to our hearts, and we choose either to stand by the word of the Lord or to go our own way. These crossroads can seem great or small, but none of them lacks significance. Our lives today are nothing more than the result of the decisions we made yesterday and all our previous days.

You are the "control center" of your life. Ultimately, if you don't fulfill your divine destiny, you can point your finger at no one else but yourself. Thus, the last dream thief I want to examine is far more personal than any other, which makes it the most powerful and seductive of all. There is a dream thief called *you*!

> You are the "control center" of your life. Ultimately, if you don't fulfill your divine destiny, you can point your finger at no one else but yourself.

DREAM THIEF NUMBER EIGHT:
YOUR OWN CHOICES

Satan desires to gain control of your soul because that's where he can influence your will — the part of you that makes choices. If the enemy can convince you that your dream is too far beyond your reach or too costly to fulfill — if he can discourage you until an attitude of defeat sets in — he knows he can keep you from fulfilling God's will for your life.

However, it's crucial to note that *Satan can't force you to do anything*! *You* are the final authority when it comes to what you choose to believe, the attitudes you choose to develop, the company you choose to keep, the way you choose to behave, and the works you choose to accomplish. Ultimately, *you* decide whether or not you will do what *you* or what *God* wants you to do — whether you will do things *your* way or *God's* way. That's why Romans 12:2 is so important. You should continuously be "...transformed by the renewing of your mind, that ye may prove what is that *good*, and *acceptable*, and *perfect*, will of God."

God exhorts us again and again to keep our minds renewed, washed, and sharpened by studying and meditating on His Word. Staying in God's Word is essential to walking out His plan and purpose for our lives. It erects a supernatural hedge of protection around our will, giving us the strength and ability to choose God's way over our way, to walk in the Spirit and not according to the flesh, and to discern between good and evil in the realm of the senses (Hebrews 5:14).

Abiding continually in the Word builds our understanding and establishes the spiritual foundation in our lives. It gives us supernatural courage to stand by a fresh word from God and launch out in faith to see it fulfilled in our lives. It enables us to come into divine alignment with His perfect plan and stand with patience until that dream comes to pass. Courage, faith, and patience flourish in our lives only because we choose them, but it is nearly impossible to choose them over our flesh and the deceptive practices of the devil if we don't abide in God's Word (*see* John 8:31,32).

David wrote in Psalm 119:11, "Thy word have I hid in mine heart, that I might not sin against thee." The greatest sin of all, and the "father" of all sin, is the sin of Adam in the Garden of Eden. Instead of fulfilling his mandate from God that would lead to his divine destiny, Adam simply decided to do what he wanted to do.

> Courage, faith, and patience flourish in our lives only because we choose them, but it is nearly impossible to choose them over our flesh and the deceptive practices of the devil if we don't abide in God's Word.

The pure and complete reversal of Adam's transgression — who, inspired by Satan, chose his own way over God's way — occurred in the Garden of Gethsemane. In that garden, the agony Jesus suffered was the ultimate human agony. He had to choose to come into divine alignment with the plan of God — to put aside His personal preferences and unequivocally surrender His entire life and destiny into the hands of Almighty God.

No matter how we look at this issue, the conclusion remains the same: The true power in every one of our lives lies in *our own will*. Every day of our lives, we make choices. We can choose to go our own way, which is ultimately inspired and directed by Satan. Or we can choose to go God's way, which is always inspired and directed by the Word and the Holy Spirit.

Many times the right choices we make can seem small and insignificant, but the Word of God declares that we should never despise the "small things" (Zechariah 4:10). Those little beginnings — those tiny decisions we make every day to do the right thing — can give birth to the most incredible and awesome miracles of our lives!

A SMALL DECISION
LEADS TO A MIGHTY MIRACLE

In his gospel, John gives the account of one of Jesus' most astounding miracles. Even most unbelievers can tell you this story because it's so widely known. But the truth is, this great miracle took place because of *one small boy's simple decision* to give his lunch away instead of keeping it for himself.

> **After these things Jesus went over the sea of Galilee, which is the sea of Tiberias. And a great multitude followed him, because they saw his miracles which he did on them that were diseased. And Jesus went up into a mountain, and there he sat with his disciples. And the passover, a feast of the Jews, was nigh.**
>
> **John 6:1-4**

This was probably the largest crowd Jesus had ever attracted during the course of His ministry, and the Greek text indicates that this crowd was continuing to grow as the people followed Jesus wherever He went. Why? Because they saw His miracles!

The Greek word for "miracles" here is *semeion*, which indicates *signs and wonders* and *creative miracles*. In other words, these miracles didn't just involve the healing of headaches or the opening of deaf ears. These were spectacular, creative miracles — such as eyes forming in sockets where previously there were no eyes, limbs growing where previously there were no limbs, and bones and joints forming where previously there were none.

When Jesus finally hiked up the mountain with the 12 disciples to get some rest and relaxation, the people followed Him — and the crowd continued to grow. The Bible says that the feast of Passover was beginning the next day; therefore, many Jewish families from all over the world were converging on Jerusalem — and, coincidentally, were traveling right by the mountain where Jesus was sitting.

By this time, Jesus' miracle ministry was in full operation, and the news of His miracles was spreading through Jewish circles like wildfire. Consequently, as Jesus reclined and relaxed with His disciples, He "lifted up his eyes" and saw a massive multitude of people climbing up the mountainside to see Him.

Later in this passage of Scripture, John tells us that 5,000 men were present (v.10). However, when women and children are also considered, some Bible scholars estimate that the crowd numbered 20,000 people or more!

THE 'PROVING' OF FAITH

As this vast crowd approached Jesus and His disciples on the mountainside, Jesus turned to Philip and asked him a seemingly ridiculous question.

> **When Jesus then lifted up his eyes, and saw a great company come unto him, he saith unto Philip, Whence shall we buy bread, that these may eat? And this he said to prove him: for he himself knew what he would do.**
>
> **John 6:5,6**

Jesus asked His disciple in effect, "Hey, Philip, how much food do we have? We need to feed these people." But verse 6 says that the reason Jesus asked this question was to "prove" or to "test" Philip. Another translation of the Greek word *peiradzo*, translated "prove," would be *expose*.

Jesus asked Philip this question to *expose* any deficiency in his faith. These disciples had lived in the presence of Jesus, and they had seen Him perform every kind of creative miracle, including raising the dead. Miracles were nothing new to them. But at this moment, they were being confronted by a problem that was totally different from anything they had faced before.

Whenever we're confronted with a new problem in our lives, that problem has a way of exposing any deficiency in our faith and accentuating any weak area in our lives. For instance, in Chapter Two, we discussed how the failure to *"maintain or hold fast"* is a symptom of a person being out of divine alignment.

All of us who are children of God have experienced the life-changing, miracle-working power of God in our lives. In the days just following our new birth, we saw God's sovereign protection and provision supernaturally at work in our lives, guarding us and tenderly caring for us as newborn babes in Christ. However, as we grew up in God and were confronted with new problems and challenges, we may have thought, *This isn't like those other problems I faced when I was a new Christian. I know that God helped me through those past situations — but this is so entirely different!* Such challenges are opportunities for our faith to be *proven* and for any deficiencies to be *exposed*. They allow us to deal with our weak areas so we can come out of the experience stronger in our walk with God.

As Jesus reclined with His disciples in the lush grass, faced with a completely new challenge, He knew exactly what He was going to do (v. 6). This fact should be a great comfort to all of us, because it lets us know that Jesus *always* knows what He's going to do. Nothing catches Him off-guard. He is always ready to release His miracle-working power into the most challenging of circumstances.

> Challenges are opportunities for our faith to be *proven* and for any deficiencies to be *exposed*. They allow us to deal with our weak areas so we can come out of the experience stronger in our walk with God.

Nevertheless, when Jesus asked Philip for an answer to the dilemma they faced, Philip didn't consider a supernatural solution. In verse 7, we see this disciple begin to "grasp at straws," looking for a way to solve this problem through natural means (like many of us often do when faced with a dilemma!).

Philip answered him, Two hundred pennyworth of bread is not sufficient for them, that every one of them may take a little.

But notice in verses 8 and 9 that the disciple Andrew shows at least a glimmer of faith. Andrew tells Jesus about a small boy in the crowd who has a small amount of food that he might share with the rest of the people.

> **One of his disciples, Andrew, Simon Peter's brother, saith unto him, there is a lad here, which hath five barley loaves, and two small fishes: BUT WHAT ARE THEY AMONG SO MANY?**

The fact that Andrew brought this lad with five loaves and two fishes to Jesus' attention indicates that this disciple must have had a degree of faith for a miracle in this situation. A small boy's lunch wasn't going to feed that enormous crowd! However, when we look at what the Greek text actually says this young boy's lunch consisted of, we understand more clearly why Andrew quickly followed up his statement with the comment, "...But what are they among so many?"

The Greek word translated "barley loaves" is *krethinos*. This barley loaf was the most fragile of breads. In fact, a more accurate translation of *krethinos* would be barley *crackers*. Furthermore, *krethinos* was called the bread of the poor; rich people didn't eat this kind of barley loaves. As for the "two small fishes," this phrase refers to pickled fish that were smaller than a sardine — about the size of a minnow.

Can you imagine the disciples' reaction to Andrew's statement? They were probably amazed that he would even mention such a stupid idea. Five crackers and two minnows for so many people! *But Jesus knew what He was going to do!*

AT YOUR CROSSROADS, CHOOSE THE MIRACLE

You see, Jesus knew that Jehovah Jireh, the Great Provider, was on the scene to supply His every need. And as Jesus held the loaves and fishes in His hands and began to distribute them, we can only imagine the joy He experienced as He illustrated the grace and provision of God through this miracle of multiplication.

> **And Jesus said, Make the men sit down. Now there was much grass in the place. So the men sat down, in number about five thousand. And Jesus took the loaves; and when he had given thanks, he distributed to the disciples, and the disciples to them that were set down; and likewise of the fishes as much as they would. When they were filled, he said unto his disciples, Gather up the fragments that remain, that nothing be lost. Therefore they gathered them together, and filled twelve baskets with the fragments of the five barley loaves, which remained over and above unto them that had eaten.**
>
> **John 6:10-13**

And let's not forget that there is more to this story than a miracle of multiplication. There is also the matter that five loaves and two fishes were obtained from a small boy. Let's face it — this one little boy had the authority to stop this miracle from happening. Those crackers and little fish were *his* snack, his personal stash. It's possible that his parents didn't even know he had packed them away to enjoy somewhere along the road to Jerusalem. And if you've ever had anything to do with little boys and their secret, personal property, you know that nothing short of a miracle will cause them to give up *their* things!

Here's another point to think about: If the boy had refused to give Jesus his five crackers and two minnows, he wouldn't have faced any condemnation. They were *his* crackers and fish. This little boy had planned ahead and had been a wise steward, "saving" for this occasion. He had every right to keep his crackers and fishes.

It's the nature of children — and adults — to hold on to their "crackers"! Often they've worked or planned for those crackers, and they consider those crackers *theirs*! That isn't necessarily considered a selfish perspective either — that is, until Jesus comes along and asks, "May I please have those crackers, even though you treasure them and deem them rightfully yours?"

That's when the protests begin: "But, Lord, I've saved and believed and sacrificed to have these crackers! Please don't ask me to give them up! Please!"

This is our crossroads. This is where we agonize in our souls as God requires us to relinquish everything we are, everything we own, everything we hope to be or to possess — and to give it all to Him. This is the power of the will: Not only do we choose our destiny, but we also decide whether or not we will walk the road of the extraordinary and the miraculous with Jesus.

The little boy could have refused Jesus and eaten his small, precious snack. In that case, the boy would have been perfectly satisfied and content for a few moments — and Jesus, because He *is* Jesus, would have blessed the boy in whatever way He could bless him.

Jesus would surely have understood if the little boy had repeated Andrew's question, "What is this among so many?" After all, why should he give up his small snack, since it was impossible for such a tiny amount of food to feed a multitude anyway? Why not go ahead and satisfy his hunger for the moment?

> **This is the power of the will: Not only do we choose our destiny, but we also decide whether or not we will walk the road of the extraordinary and the miraculous with Jesus.**

Think of the tragedy of missing such a great miracle of God because of self-consumption — and yet many of us do it all the time. Isn't it remarkable how important our property becomes to us? And so often we don't think of our contribution as small until God asks for it! Our "five crackers and two minnows" often seem so great and wonderful to us until God asks for them. Then suddenly, they seem "so little among so many" — when the truth is, we just don't want to relinquish them to the Lord for His use!

In 1991, God spoke to my heart and said, "Rick, I want you to pack up and move your family to the Soviet Union."

My first response (but, thank God, not my last!) was, "But, Lord, who am I among so many?"

There are many Bible examples of God using someone or something that seemed insignificant. For instance, when Israel needed a mighty deliverer to storm Pharaoh's court and lead the Hebrews out of Egypt, He sent a tiny baby boy, floating in a basket along the bank of the Nile River.

And when the children of Israel stood before the raging Red Sea with the army of Pharaoh thundering behind them, what did God tell Moses? "Hit the water with your rod, Moses." Imagine what Moses would have forfeited if, rather than obeying the Lord, he had protested, "But, God, what is this rod among so many Egyptian soldiers and chariots?"

When Jesus received the five crackers and two minnows and then fed many thousands of people with this tiny meal, the disciples and the multitude were utterly astounded and blessed by the miracle. But no one felt the level of joy and satisfaction that the little boy who gave his lunch must have experienced. As this boy walked through the crowd, watching the people eat until their sides hurt, he must have thought to himself with a sense of awe, *Those used to be my crackers and my fishes!*

No one in the crowd was aware of the exhilaration this young lad felt because this miracle of provision had begun with him. That little boy's heart must have leapt within him to realize that when he placed his few precious crackers and two little minnows in Jesus' hands, he had chosen a miracle for his life!

GOD'S ULTIMATE PURPOSE

At the end of this account, we discover the end result of the miracle Jesus performed that day on the mountainside:

> **Then those men, when they had seen the miracle that Jesus did, said, This is of a truth that prophet that should come into the world.**
>
> John 6:14

This verse is saying that when the people saw Jesus perform this miracle of multiplication, they received a new revelation of who He was. In the same way, the issue in our lives is not just the relinquishing of our hold on our money, time, or talent — *the issue is our willingness to move into a new realm with God!* We give Jesus our time, our finances, our possessions, our businesses, and our talents — and then we watch Him multiply our gifts both for our good and for the good of the multitudes. But the final result — and our ultimate joy — is that, in the end, we receive a fresh illumination of our Lord and Savior, as do the people whose lives we have touched.

> Choosing to walk in God's supernatural presence and tap into His miracle-working power often means we must step out of our safe, warm boat and onto the tumultuous waves of a stormy sea in order to walk toward Jesus.

To achieve that point of revelation, however, we sometimes have to make difficult and even frightening choices. Choosing to walk in God's supernatural presence and tap into His miracle-working power often means we must step out of our safe, warm boat and onto the tumultuous waves of a stormy sea in order to walk toward Jesus.

Each time we reach a crossroads in life, a word comes from Heaven that challenges our faith. God asks us to do something different, and His new assignment always exposes our comfort zone — the rut we've been living in that has become all too familiar and secure. More often than not, we like where we are because, if nothing else, it's familiar. But as the Holy Spirit moves us from place to place, from task to task, and from challenge to challenge, He wants us to understand that *He alone* is to be our comfort zone!

Not only must you allow God to deal with your "comfort zones," but you must also face head-on the "What-am-I-among-so-many?" mentality. That mentality is one of the dream thieves that will keep you from fulfilling the plan of God for your life.

> Give the little you have to Jesus, placing all that you are and all that you possess in His hands. Then trust Him to be Himself, and you will see the miracle of multiplication!

When the Lord asks you to do something, don't compare yourself and your abilities to the need you are called to meet. If that's the perspective you choose to focus on, you'll never move beyond your status quo. Instead, give the little you have to Jesus, placing all that you are and all that you possess in His hands. Then trust Him to be Himself, and you will see the miracle of multiplication! Your small contribution can feed a multitude. The healing love and understanding you show one person can multiply into an international ministry to the suffering. As you willingly give your gift to God for the sake of others, their own gifts will blossom in their lives and return multiplied blessings to your life beyond anything you could ever imagine!

DON'T MISS YOUR MIRACLE!

"Pack up your family and move to the Soviet Union, Rick!"

With that one word from God, every deficiency in my spiritual life came rushing to the forefront! But when I began to release all I had into the hands of Jesus — when I chose to stand and face the dream thieves until all of them were defeated — that deficiency was swallowed up by the miracle power of God.

Yes, we could have had kept our "crackers and minnows." We could have stayed in the United States and enjoyed a good life and a growing stateside ministry. *But if we had chosen that course, we would have missed the miracle of the ministry God had for our family in the former Soviet Union.*

Denise and I knew we could *not* miss the miracle God had in store for our lives! We simply couldn't live the rest of our lives wondering what would have been accomplished if we had obeyed God — wondering how much richer and more intimate our relationship with God would have been had we walked in His perfect will. The very idea of standing one day before the Judgment Seat of Christ and having Jesus show us a full-length movie of everything we missed by choosing to go our own way was, and always will be, a devastating and grievous thought to our hearts.

To me, there is no greater tragedy than missing the miracle, and I'll tell you why. If you refuse the miracle and choose what seems to be the "safe" road, you will still be God's child, and He will still bless you as much as He can. You can still believe in Him, pray to Him, and even endeavor to please Him in all that you do. But you will never really come to know Jesus the way you could have if you had dared to believe and obey.

> Denise and I couldn't live the rest of our lives wondering what would have been accomplished if we had obeyed God — wondering how much richer and more intimate our relationship with God would have been had we walked in His perfect will.

Here is the most incredible and remarkable part of this process: As you obey Jesus' voice and follow His plan, giving all that you are into His hands, you are changed into His image. Step by step, you get to know Him more intimately than ever before as you grow more and more like the One you are following. So I ask you:

- Are you holding back some part of your life that you know God is asking you to relinquish to Him?

- Are you going through the motions in your Christian experience, but falling short in developing an intimate relationship with the Father?

- What is the Master asking of you today? Is He asking you to "launch out into the deep"? Or is He asking you to embrace your dream with renewed faith and patience as you wait upon Him?

Don't ignore any crossroads, great or small, for these are the pathways God is clearing for you to step into your dream!

God's ultimate purpose was not just to get an ark built or to deliver Israel out of bondage in Egypt. Ultimately, He didn't just want the ark; He wanted Noah's heart and soul. In the same way, God just didn't just want to free a few million Israelites so He could call them His own personal nation. He wanted an intimate rela-

> Don't ignore any crossroads, great or small, for these are the pathways God is clearing for you to step into your dream!

tionship with a people whose hearts and souls were freely and gratefully given to Him.

Likewise, when God reveals to you His plan and purpose for your life, His ultimate purpose is that, through obeying Him and walking in His Word, you will enter into holy communion with Him. This is the greatest miracle of all and one that I personally couldn't live without.

You could say that I am totally, unalterably, and irreversibly addicted to the presence of God! Every pore of my being cries out for more knowledge of God and of His ways, His thoughts, and His feelings. There is nothing more sacred to me and nothing I covet more than my personal relationship with Him.

At times I've considered the irony of what we often say when we see a believer choosing to go his own way instead of God's way: "Well, he missed God on that one!" But there's more truth to that statement than meets the eye! When we decide to go our own way, we forfeit an intimate knowledge of and relationship with our Heavenly Father. We truly do miss God and His will for our lives.

It is the most profoundly astonishing fact that, as we tenaciously and passionately *hold fast to*, *cling to*, and *stand by* all the dreams Jesus has placed in our hearts, we find ourselves face to face with Him — His majesty, His magnificent power, and His unfathomable love. When we come to each crossroad in our lives, Jesus is reason enough to declare to ourselves and to every dream thief that would keep His light from dispelling our darkness: "With all my heart, soul, mind, and strength, *I choose the miracle*!"

THINK ABOUT IT

Everyone faces crossroads in life. Each crossroad is significant because it requires you to make a decision, and your decisions direct your course. Ultimately, they determine the destination and final outcome of your life.

Do you detect a negative pattern in your life? You are the only common denominator that you can control. Change your choices, and you'll automatically change your results.

Your will is the control center of your life. You can shape and influence your own will to gravitate toward God and toward what is good by filling your mind and your mouth with the Word of God and with truth. What occupies your mind will penetrate your heart — and there, at the seat of your will, your choices will be made.

What occupies your thought life on a regular basis? What habits occupy your time in private? Your answer will indicate the direction in which your will is steering your life. If you don't like the destination you see on the horizon, now is a good time to make some changes and shift your focus so you won't sabotage your own dream by taking a detour that leads to a dead end.

Life is filled with crossroads. You can choose a path that's "okay" or one that is *extraordinary*. How will you know the difference? The path that God invites you to travel may contain challenges and difficulties. Yet it will also cause you to rely on Him, to grow up in Him, and, ultimately, to produce the excellence and character that can only be forged by His work in your life.

PRAYER OF SALVATION

When Jesus Christ comes into your life, you are immediately emancipated — totally set free from the bondage of sin!

If you have never received Jesus as your personal Savior, it is time to experience this new life for yourself! The first step to freedom is simple. Just pray this prayer from your heart:

Lord, I can never adequately thank You for all You did for me on the Cross. I am so undeserving, Jesus, but You came and gave Your life for me anyway. I repent and turn from my sins right now, Jesus. I receive You as my Savior, and I ask You to wash away my sin by Your precious blood. I thank You from the depths of my heart for doing what no one else could do for me. Had it not been for Your willingness to lay down Your life for me, I would be eternally lost.

Thank You, Jesus, that I am now redeemed by Your blood. You bore my sin, my sickness, my pain, my lack of peace, and my suffering on the Cross. Your blood has cleansed me from my sin and washed me whiter than snow, giving me rightstanding with the Father. I have no need to be ashamed of my past sins, because I am now a new creature in You. Old things have passed away, and all things have become new because I am in Jesus Christ (1 Corinthians 5:17).

Because of You, Jesus, today I am forgiven; I am filled with peace; and I am a joint heir with You! Satan no longer has a right to lay any claim on me. From a grateful heart, I will faithfully serve You the rest of my days!

If you prayed this prayer from your heart, something amazing has happened to you. No longer a servant to sin, you are now a servant of Almighty God. The evil spirits that once exacted every ounce of your being and required your all-inclusive servitude no longer possess the authorization to control you or to dictate your destiny.

As a result of your decision to turn your life over to Jesus Christ, your eternal home has been decided forever. HEAVEN is now your permanent address.

God's Spirit has moved into your own human spirit, and you have become the "temple of God" (1 Corinthians 6:19). What a miracle! To think that God, by His Spirit, now lives inside of you! I have never ceased to be amazed at this incredible miracle of God in my own life. He gave me (and you!) a new heart and then made us His home!

Now you have a new Lord and Master, and His name is Jesus. From this moment on, the Spirit of God will work in you and supernaturally energize you to fulfill God's will for your life. Everything will change for you now — and it's all going to change for the best!

REFERENCE BOOK LIST

1. *How To Use New Testament Greek Study Aids* by Walter Jerry Clark (Loizeaux Brothers).

2. *Strong's Exhaustive Concordance of the Bible* by James H. Strong.

3. *The Interlinear Greek-English New Testament* by George Ricker Berry (Baker Book House).

4. *The Englishman's Greek Concordance of the New Testament* by George Wigram (Hendrickson).

5. *New Thayer's Greek-English Lexicon of the New Testament* by Joseph Thayer (Hendrickson).

6. *The Expanded Vine's Expository Dictionary of New Testament Words* by W. E. Vine (Bethany).

7. *New International Dictionary of New Testament Theology (DNTT)*; Colin Brown, editor (Zondervan).

8. *Theological Dictionary of the New Testament (TDNT)* by Geoffrey Bromiley; Gephard Kittle, editor (Eerdmans Publishing Co.).

9. *The New Analytical Greek Lexicon*; Wesley Perschbacher, editor (Hendrickson).

10. *The Linguistic Key to the Greek New Testament* by Fritz Rienecker and Cleon Rogers (Zondervan).

11. *Word Studies in the Greek New Testament* by Kenneth Wuest, 4 Volumes (Eerdmans).

12. *New Testament Words* by William Barclay (Westminster Press).

ABOUT THE AUTHOR

Rick Renner is a respected leader and teacher within the Christian community, both in the U.S. and abroad. He fills a unique position in the modern Christian world, combining an extraordinary depth of scriptural and practical knowledge with an easy-to-understand, faith-filled approach to the Bible. Rick became passionate about the Greek New Testament when studying Journalism and Classical Greek as a university student. In the years that followed, he continued his extensive study of the Greek New Testament, later earning a Doctor of Philosophy in Ministry.

Along with his wife Denise and their sons and families, Rick works to see the Gospel preached, leadership trained, and churches established throughout the world. Together, their global mission is to teach, strengthen, and rescue. Rick is the founder of the *Good News Television Network* (aka *Media Mir*), the first Christian television network established in the former Soviet Union that today broadcasts the Gospel to a potential audience of 110 million people. His broadcast "Good News With Rick Renner" can be seen across the entire former USSR. Rick has distributed hundreds of thousands of teaching audio and videotapes, and his best-selling books have been translated into four major languages. In addition, Rick teaches via the Internet with English-speaking broadcasts.

Rick is the founder of the *"It's Possible"* humanitarian foundation, an organization committed to providing for the practical needs of various segments of Russian society. He is also the founder of the *Good News Association of Pastors and Churches,* through which he oversees and strengthens hundreds of churches throughout the former Soviet Union. In addition, Rick and Denise pastor the thriving *Moscow Good News Church*, located in the very heart of Moscow, Russia. *RENNER Ministries* has offices in Russia, Ukraine, Latvia, England, and the United States. Rick resides in Moscow with his wife and their three sons and families.

ABOUT OUR WORK
IN THE FORMER USSR

From inception to its current role in the Body of Christ, *RENNER Ministries'* purpose and vision has been to teach, strengthen, and rescue people for the Kingdom of God. Although the Renners' ministry began much earlier, in 1991 God called Rick and Denise Renner and their family to what is now the former Soviet Union. Since that time, millions of lives have been touched by the various outreaches of *RENNER Ministries*. Nevertheless, the Renners' ever-increasing vision for this region of the world continues to expand across 11 time zones to reach 300 million precious souls for God's Kingdom.

The *Moscow Good News Church* was begun in September 2000 in the very heart of Moscow, right next to Red Square. Since that time, the church has grown to become one of the largest Protestant churches in Moscow and a strategic model for pastors throughout this region of the world to learn from and emulate. Today the outreaches of the *Moscow Good News Church* includes ministry to families, senior citizens, children, youth, and international church members, as well as a special-ized ministry to businesspeople and an outreach to the poor and needy. Rick and Denise also founded churches in Riga, Latvia, and in Kiev, Ukraine, both of which continue to thrive.

Part of the mission of *RENNER Ministries* is to come alongside pastors and ministers and take them to a higher level of excellence and professionalism in the ministry. Therefore, since 1991 when the walls of Communism first collapsed, this ministry has been working in the former USSR to train and equip pastors, church leaders, and ministers, helping them attain the necessary skills and knowledge to fulfill the ministries that the Lord has given to them.

To this end, Rick Renner founded both a seminary and a ministerial association. The *Good News Seminary* is a school that operates as a part of the *Moscow Good News Church*. It specializes in training leaders to start new churches all over the former Soviet Union. The *Good News Association of Pastors and Churches* is a church-planting and church-supporting organization with a membership of pastors and churches that numbers in the hundreds.

RENNER Ministries also owns and operates the *Good News Television Network*, the first and one of the largest TV outreaches within the territory of the former USSR. Since its inception in 1992, this television network has become one of the strongest instruments available today for declaring the Word of God to the 15 nations of the former Soviet Union, reaching 110 million potential viewers every day with the Gospel of Jesus Christ.

In addition, Rick Renner also founded the *"It's Possible!"* humanitarian foundation, which is involved in various outreaches in the city of Moscow. The *"It's Possible"* foundation uses innovative methods to help different age groups of people who are in great need.

If you would like to learn more about our work in the former Soviet Union, please visit our website at www.renner.org, or call 918-496-3213.

A NOTE TO BOOKSELLERS

For all wholesale book orders,
please contact:

TEACH ALL NATIONS

A book company anointed to take God's Word
to you and to the nations of the world.

A Division of
Rick Renner Ministries
P. O. Box 702040
Tulsa, OK 74170-2040
Phone: 877-281-8644
Fax: 918-496-3278
E-mail: tan@renner.org
Website: www.tanpublish.com

FOR FURTHER INFORMATION

For additional copies of this book
or for further information
about this ministry and other Renner products,
please contact the RENNER Ministries office nearest you,
or visit the ministry website at www.renner.org.
(**Note:** Online orders of products within the U.S. only.)

ALL USA CORRESPONDENCE:
RENNER Ministries
P. O. Box 702040
Tulsa, OK 74170-2040
(918) 496-3213
Or 1-800-RICK-593
E-mail: renner@renner.org
Website: www.renner.org

MOSCOW OFFICE:
RENNER Ministries
P. O. Box 53
Moscow 109316, Russia
7 (095) 727-1470
E-mail: mirpress@umail.ru
Website: www.mgnc.org

RIGA OFFICE:
RENNER Ministries
Unijas 99
Riga LV-1084, Latvia
(371) 780-2150
E-mail: info@goodnews.lv

KIEV OFFICE:
RENNER Ministries
P. O. Box 146
Kiev, 01025, Ukraine
380 (44) 246-6552
E-mail: mirpress@rrm.kiev.ua

OXFORD OFFICE:
RENNER Ministries
Box 7, 266 Banbury Road
Oxford OX2 7DL, England
44 (1865) 355509
E-mail: europe@renner.org

Mining the Treasures of God's Word

Author Rick Renner unearths a rich treasure trove of truths in his remarkable devotional, ***Sparkling Gems From the Greek***. Drawing from an extensive study of both the Bible and New Testament Greek, Rick illuminates 365 passages with more than 1,285 in-depth Greek word studies. Far from intellectualizing, he blends his solid instruction with practical applications and refreshing insights. Find challenge, reassurance, comfort, and reminders of God's abiding love and healing every day of the year.

$34.95 (Hardback)
ISBN: 978-0-9725454-2-6

Sparkling Gems From the Greek Electronic Reference Edition

Now you are only a few short clicks away from discovering the untold riches of God's Word! Offering embedded links to three exhaustive indices for ultimate ease in cross-referencing scriptures and Greek word studies, this unique computer study tool gives you both convenience and portability as you read and explore Rick Renner's one-of-a-kind daily devotional!

ISBN: 978-0-9725454-7-1   **$29.95** (CD-ROM)

A Biblical Approach to Spiritual Warfare

Rick Renner's book *Dressed To Kill* is considered by many to be a true classic on the subject of scriptural warfare. The original version, which sold more than 400,000 copies, is a curriculum staple in Bible schools worldwide. In this beautifully bound hardback volume, you will find:

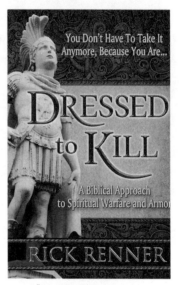

- 512 pages of reedited text
- 16 pages of full-color illustrations
- Questions at the end of each chapter to guide you into deeper study

In *Dressed To Kill*, Rick explains with exacting detail the purpose and function of each piece of Roman armor. In the process, he describes the

$24.95 (Hardback)
ISBN: 978-0-9779459-0-0

significance of our *spiritual* armor not only to withstand the onslaughts of the enemy and but also to overturn the tendencies of the carnal mind. Furthermore, Rick delivers a clear, scriptural presentation on the biblical definition of spiritual warfare — what it is and what it is not.

When you walk with God in deliberate, continual fellowship, He will enrobe you with Himself. Armed with the knowledge of who you are in Him, you will be dressed and dangerous to the works of darkness, unflinching in the face of conflict, and fully equipped to take the offensive and gain mastery over any opposition from your spiritual foe. You don't have to accept defeat anymore once you are *dressed to kill*!

BOOKS BY RICK RENNER